DISCARD

RELIGION AND
IMAGINATION

'We can only set right one error of expression by another. By this method of antagonism we steady our minds . . . by saying and unsaying to a positive result.'

J. H. NEWMAN

RELIGION AND IMAGINATION

'*in aid of a grammar of assent*'

BY

JOHN COULSON

CLARENDON PRESS · OXFORD

1981

Oxford University Press, Walton Street, Oxford OX2 6DP
London Glasgow New York Toronto
Delhi Bombay Calcutta Madras Karachi
Kuala Lumpur Singapore Hong Kong Tokyo
Nairobi Dar es Salaam Cape Town
Melbourne Wellington
and associate companies in
Beirut Berlin Ibadan Mexico City

Published in the United States by
Oxford University Press, New York

© John Coulson 1981

All rights reserved. No part of this publication may be reproduced,
stored in a retrieval system, or transmitted, in any form or by any means,
electronic, mechanical, photocopying, recording, or otherwise, without
the prior permission of Oxford University Press

British Library Cataloguing in Publication Data

Coulson, John
Religion and imagination.
1. Imagination
2. Religion and literature
3. English literature — 19th century — History and criticism
4. English literature — 20th century — History and criticism
I. Title
820'.9'008   PR468.14   80-41355

ISBN 0-19-826656-1

Typeset by Oxprint Ltd., Oxford
Printed in Great Britain
at the University Press, Oxford
by Eric Buckley
Printer to the University

Preface

The purpose of this book is to show what the student and teacher of religion may gain from cultivating a properly imaginative response to literature in general, and to the writers discussed in particular. The reader of literature may also find it helpful to see how familiar texts fit into an unfamiliar but related argument.

The argument is that questions about belief, such as how religious propositions are true, cannot be either simply put or simply resolved. They can be put properly only as the conditions and limits imposed by the ways in which we actually hold our beliefs are observed. Before we can explain or justify them, beliefs are held in faith; and we discover that, as a condition of their successful justification, they must first be credible to imagination. Thus the questions about belief which can be resolved have the form: how can I believe what I cannot understand or absolutely prove? How does an impression on the imagination become a creed or system in the reason?

This is so because what we hold in faith is most frequently expressed in metaphor, symbol, and story and, as such, prior to and as a condition of its verification, it requires an imaginative assent comparable to that we give to poems and novels.

To understand how religion and imagination are related to each other, the most effective method is to concentrate upon the traditional overlap of religion and literature. But in so doing we must anticipate an objection—that such a relationship is plausible only in an age of faith, now superseded, since conditions arise after the age of Shakespeare which inevitably invert the priorities: faith becomes conditional upon understanding.

This question, in the form proposed in Part One, is answered by Newman. In Part Two it is reconsidered from a more radical standpoint, imaginatively and theologically—that of Feuerbach and the writers who, although in some cases contemporary with Newman, conceived themselves to be between two incompatible worlds. They despaired of being able to hold beliefs in circumstances which, by the end of the nineteenth century, appeared to be *uniquely* different from those in which they had originated. How radically have the questions changed? Does a great divide separate us irreversibly from our past? Or does a grammar common to faith and belief, and thus to poet and theologian, still exist and have application? An answer emerges as Newman's theological argument in Part One is related to T. S. Eliot's poetic achievement in resolving the dilemma expressed by the poets, novelists, and theologians considered in Part Two.

ACKNOWLEDGEMENTS

The material of this book derives from two separate but related fields of study. The initial impetus was given by an Anglo-American symposium on method in the study of literature and theology held at Boston College, Mass., in 1969, and made possible by the generosity of the Danforth Foundation and by the enthusiasm of my collaborator, Professor Joseph Appleyard, SJ, to whom I express my gratitude. I also owe much to the subsequent inter-departmental seminar at Bristol University, out of which has grown the special degree of Religion with Literature. I wish to thank colleagues and students in the two Departments, of Theology and English, and Professor Christopher Ricks for his vigorous criticisms and encouragement. Some of this material was broadcast in a series of programmes on Religion and Literature by the BBC in 1975.

As the sub-title indicates, the theological emphasis falls upon John Henry Newman, and I am especially grateful to the Superior and members of the Birmingham Oratory for so kindly allowing me to investigate and publish material from their archives. The section on Newman was read and approved by Fr. Stephen Dessain just before his untimely death, and I wish to record my deep obligation to him for his unfailing kindness and criticism. The development of this section has been pursued in papers contributed to successive International Newman symposia at Luxembourg, Freiburg, Dublin, and Rome. Part has been published in the *Times Literary Supplement*, *Concilium*, and the *Downside Review*: while the chapter on Newman and Maurice was contributed to the F. D. Maurice Centenary Conference at Trinity Hall, Cambridge in 1972.

It was correspondence with the late Professor Maurice Nédoncelle which encouraged me to begin this book, and its writing was made possible by my appointment, first to a Downside Research Fellowship, and then to a Lectureship at Bristol University, whose assistance I most gratefully acknowledge. The detailed criticism and unremitting encouragement I have received from the Revd Canon F. W. Dillistone, Emeritus Fellow of Oriel College, Oxford, has helped me to deal with problems as they arose, and it is a special pleasure to record my particular indebtedness to him. I have also been most fortunate in receiving much help from my publishers.

Of those who have read parts of the manuscript and given me invaluable advice, I should like to thank in particular the Revd Gabriel Daly, Mr Richard Giddens, Mr Gerard Kilroy, Professor Nicholas Lash, Dom Illtyd Trethowan, the Rt. Revd John Tinsley, and Sr. Paulette Toth. My thanks are also due to Mr and Mrs John Farrell for making the index, and to Mrs Anne Cade and Mrs Peggy Gullidge for typing the manuscript. In conclusion, I wish to express, however inadequately, my gratitude to my wife, Violet Coulson, for her unfailing support.

Bristol   JOHN COULSON
April 1980

Contents

Abbreviations

(for full titles and particulars, see Bibliography)

Apo.	J. H. Newman, *Apologia pro Vita Sua*, the two versions of 1864 and 1865, ed. W. Ward.
Arians	J. H. Newman, *The Arians of the Fourth Century*.
BL	S. T. Coleridge, *Biographia Literaria*.
BN	T. S. Eliot, *Four Quartets, Burnt Norton*.
CN	S. T. Coleridge, *The Notebooks*, ed. Kathleen Coburn.
DA	J. H. Newman, *Discussions and Arguments*.
Dev.	J. H. Newman, *An Essay on the Development of Christian Doctrine*, ed. C. F. Harrold.
DS	T. S. Eliot, *Four Quartets, The Dry Salvages*.
EC	T. S. Eliot, *Four Quartets, East Coker*.
ECH	J. H. Newman, *Essays Critical and Historical*.
GA	J. H. Newman, *An Essay in aid of a Grammar of Assent*, ed. C. F. Harrold.
Letters	J. H. Newman, *The Letters and Diaries of John Henry Newman*, ed. C. S. Dessain.
LG	T. S. Eliot, *Four Quartets, Little Gidding*.
Lit. Rem.	S. T. Coleridge, *The Literary Remains*, ed. H. N. Coleridge.
M.	J. B. Mozley, 'Bishop Andrewes' Sermons'.
N.	J. H. Newman, *The Philosophical Notebook*.
O	J. H. Newman, Symbol used to differentiate unpublished from published material in the archives of Birmingham Oratory.
OPP	T. S. Eliot, *On Poetry and Poets*.
OUS	J. H. Newman, *Fifteen Sermons preached before the University of Oxford*.
PPS	J. H. Newman, *Parochial and Plain Sermons*.
SE	T. S. Eliot, *Selected Essays* (1969 edn.)
Sub.	F. D. Maurice, *Subscription No Bondage*.
T	J. H. Newman, *The Theological Papers*.
VM	J. H. Newman, *The Via Media of the Anglican Church*.

PART ONE

IMAGINATION
AND BELIEF

The Priority of Imagination

(I) RELIGION AND LITERATURE

> A verse may finde him who a sermon flies
> And turn delight into a sacrifice.
>
> GEORGE HERBERT

The mutual dependence of religious awareness and imagination is recognized for what it is only as each begins to go its own way. This—a phenomenon of the West and of the past hundred years in particular—has had disastrous consequences for religion. When the vital connection between religion and imagination is either overlooked or denied, it is not merely theology or the theologian that suffers. The very life of religion ebbs and becomes infertile. During the past century, religion has gradually ceased to be part of the literary culture and, in that sense of the term, the theologian has become 'un-lettered'. His subject-matter, no longer taken for granted culturally, is not thought to be fitted for general study as part of a liberal education. Instead, he has laboured in seminary confinement, and become the prisoner of his theological explanations, which are sharply defined, unmysterious, and rigid.

Conversely, the questions which the reading of literature puts to religion have the supreme merit of being *unforced* and spontaneous. When compared with those which theologians put to each other or which apologists extract from unwilling school children, such questions do not at first appear to be 'theological', since they lack that 'contrived' and 'notional' characteristic which the nature of the subject seems to require. This is because, under inevitable theological pressure, religion is always being reduced to notions. We have continually to revise our abstractions, and to ask: is our God too small?

This is most forcibly brought home to the layman when he suddenly realizes that a sermon he has just heard is not in the same class as a novel he has just finished for moral insight: 'a verse may finde him who a sermon flies'. It is then that we understand why it may be asserted that it is in what a work of

literature successfully achieves that our religious insights are
not only realized but themselves are judged. To what extent can
a belief be said to be established as true, if it has failed to
convince or to be successfully brought alive and made real?
Religious belief may claim to authenticate our experiences, but
must not authentication wait upon conviction?

It has, of course, been argued that religious beliefs are self-
authenticating, and that they are most truly expressed when
most sharply opposed to the prevailing culture. This is a one-
sided view of religion. If anything, history asserts the contrary.
When a religious claim ceases to find convincing embodiment
or ground in its contemporary culture, it soon degenerates into
an implausible rhetoric. A saint may move directly from the
Sermon on the Mount to politics—that is his privilege—but the
power of a religion to authenticate its beliefs is normally at its
greatest when they shine through or are mediated by the arts,
politics, and other forms of social intercourse. Although most
people have a faith, they do not necessarily like to have it
named. They prefer to meet it incognito. Their beliefs are often
most convincingly expressed when they are given secular meanings and, in particular, when they are successfully translated
into the language of literary imagination.

In so doing, a literature does more than 'reflect' the beliefs by
which a community lives. In bringing the character of our
engagement with them vividly to the surface of consciousness, it
'realizes' them, often for the first time. Suddenly we gain that
sharpness of focus which makes us understand how 'notional'
our assent has been until that moment. 'What oft was thought,
but ne'er so well expressed' is still one criterion of literary
success, so that when what we profess is confronted by the
reality of what literature reveals, the shock waves do not last for
long. The secret imaginings of one generation become the
common property of the next who forget, for example, that
D. H. Lawrence was judged to be a pornographer, or that the
then Bishop of Wakefield burned his copy of Hardy's *Jude the
Obscure*.

What the study of literature does, particularly that of nine-
teenth-century literature, is to reveal the *form* of the questions
which *should* have concerned theologians, but did not—with one
exception. Of our major theologians, it is J. H. Newman who

pre-eminently grasps the form our questions should take if the ancient relationship between belief and imagination is to be restored or realized anew. But it must be a Newman approached by means of our questions today, and interpreted within their pressure. For example, as between ourselves and the age of Shakespeare, there has been a change of consciousness. Is it unique and irreversible? And must our beliefs be rationally verified *before* they may be held, or can we still hold what we cannot satisfactorily explain? Forms of faith continue to exist which are more rudimentary than articles or propositions of belief. They are preserved in metaphor, analogue, symbol, and myth—forms which are also those of literary imagination. Have they been superseded chronologically? Or should our beliefs still first be credible to imagination before they may be tested by reason? If so, how are religious propositions 'true'; and how may we become certain of what we cannot absolutely 'prove'?

Newman's published writings, if read in the light of his notebooks, letters, and other manuscripts, are capable of much greater expansion and application to such questions than is commonly supposed, even by Newman scholars. This is particularly true of that 'essay in aid of a grammar of assent' which is, as I shall show, a main source of the theological framework (or grammar) within which T.S. Eliot achieves the poetry of *Four Quartets*. Eliot's poetry exemplifies what Newman's theology explains.

In matters of affirmation and belief, religion and literature continue to overlap. What is sometimes overlooked is that literary criticism seems to assume a higher threshold of acceptance than biblical exegesis: to subject a Shakespeare text to the rigours of contemporary New Testament criticism, for example, would lead to its immediate evaporation. And when the Bible is translated or the liturgy is recast in language insensitive to the literary forms of scripture, this is further evidence of the extent to which theologians have lost touch with those imaginative assents without which literary criticism, as we know it, could not be practised. Classical literary texts are authentic 'scriptures', that is, they require and justify an imaginative assent and, by so requiring and justifying, they teach us the nature of such assents.

In revealing the form of the questions which should have concerned theologians, literature also conserves. What it 'realizes' may be beliefs and certitudes which philosophers (and theologians) have lost the art to verify: whether it be the *modesty* of a Desdemona or Cordelia; the *honour* which continues to elude a Macbeth hell-bent upon success; or 'the noxious smell untraceable in the drains'. This may be why literary critics are more hesitant than philosophers and theologians to accept the claims of a society which asserts the break with its past, ethically as well as religiously, to be unique and irreversible. Can values be totally 'trans-valued', or is this, Nietzsche's claim, merely a rhetorical device for objecting to simple or customary forms of continuity? When Harvey Cox, for example, in *The Secular City*, deprecates the theology and social relationships of the pre-industrial village, in favour of the anonymous, functional relationships of the big city, is what he is recommending a radical, but inevitable, theological change, or merely an impoverished sensibility? We may fail to recognize that the present must be relativized as well as the past, and that our perception of 'reality' is of what we 'half-create'. This, the overwhelming testimony of poets and novelists, is to claim that what we are determines what we perceive—'a fool sees not the same tree that a wise man sees'—and that the world of 'imagination' is more not less 'real' than that either of the energetic ecclesiastical administrator or of our own unawakened selves.

(II) COLERIDGE ON RELIGION AND IMAGINATION

Then I asked: 'does a firm persuasion that a thing is so, make is so?'
He replied: 'All poets believe that it does, & in ages of imagination this firm persuasion removed mountains.'

WILLIAM BLAKE, *The Marriage of Heaven and Hell*

The term 'imagination' is one to which the maxim: 'Don't ask for the meaning, ask for the use', pre-eminently applies. Its use in literary criticism (as in theology) is to denote a particular kind of cognitive perception. It marks the arousal of a state of deep but highly ordered feeling, which is never mere feeling but has as its object a new sense of reality. When Coleridge, for example, speaks of imagination as what brings the whole soul of man into activity, it may seem that an appeal to imagination is to a distinct mental faculty. Philosophically this is a trap to be avoided: it blurs the stages of imaginative articulation. Imagination is not one faculty and reason another. Otherwise, by being obliged to define what we mean by 'imagination' we end up with nothing better than the power to picture or visualize—a power notoriously confined to an unreliable minority. An appeal to imagination is made when an explanation has fallen short. It begins as a criticism—as 'this is not what I meant', or 'I meant more', as when Pascal, for example, points out that the God of the philosophers is imaginatively inadequate to the God of Abraham and Isaac. When we dismiss a belief as unreal, abstract, or fixated, we are on the brink of appealing to imagination, as to a way of seeing something differently or in a new light. This is so when we are asked 'put yourself in his place', or 'turn the question round and see it from a different standpoint'. Thus, as Coleridge saw, the appeal is to a creative power, to a change of mode—to what 'dissolves, diffuses, dissipates, in order to re-create'.[1] It is this re-creative power of imagination which baffles philosophers: imagination in its full, complete, and proper form comprises the very powers of growth and production, for which no prescription or criterion can be given in advance of its successful realization. Faced by this difficulty, philosophers have often been accused of having too little sensibility, or of rejoicing in a lack of imagination; but it remains, philosophically, the most prudent course to conceive imagination negatively, as a qualifier, rather than substantively: it is a clearing of the ground, a freeing from false conceptions and narrow views. But it is when we turn to literature and to such writers as Shakespeare, Dostoevsky, and T. S. Eliot that we realize to what extent such prudence confines us to the foothills of human experience. It is literature which shows us that we cannot rest in a purely negative conception of imagination. It does more than suspend our disbelief. It predisposes us to believe in what it has realized. Not only is this obviously so when we respond to the great writers; but it is also true of the demands made upon us by the primary forms of religious faith. Expressed as they are in metaphor, symbol, and story, these too require a similar response. What is more they are the 'first-order' forms by which the adequacy of our 'second-order' beliefs or philosophical notions is judged.

[1] *BL*, chap. xiii.

What puts Hume in his place, with his talk about apprentice deities having made an imperfect world, is the *whole* tragic imagination of Shakespeare and its resolution in *The Tempest* and the Last Plays. Similarly, a naïve conception of the deity as a benign clockmaker splits on the rock of our experience of evil, in the trial and death of Jesus, or as Lear is destroyed by his daughters. It is an abnormal person who has never known one moment of fear and trembling in which his torpid, even-tempered world erupts in passion, accident, or death. For an instant he sees his condition as that of being out over 70,000 fathoms; and then, once more, imagination sleeps in the unconscious:

> Most souls, 'tis true, but peep out once an age,
> Dull, sullen pris'ners in the body's cage:
> Dim lights of life, that burn a length of years,
> Useless, unseen, as lamps in sepulchres.[2]

When we 'use imagination', we begin to see our world differently. Our standpoint or focus changes, but this act of imagination remains incomplete until spontaneously and creatively we gain an enlarged sense of reality. But our powers of perception are more than merely enlarged. They are reordered. In literature the imagination of a Shakespeare or a Dostoevsky succeeds, as it deals with diversities of character and incident, in bringing about 'a more than usual state of emotion with more than usual order';[3] and its arousal—in play, novel, or poem—helps us to recognize and even, by analogy, 'to elicit some perception of an order in reality'.

On this view, literary achievement is not self-authenticating, autonomous, or merely 'aesthetic'. Instead, it is expressive of values which, although related to and uniquely expressible in literature, are also expressible ethically—in a manner or style of life. This is a position still asserted by F. R. Leavis and L. C. Knights. The critical vocabulary derives from Coleridge, as do the distinctions presuming a relationship between pleasure and truth, conviction and authentication. Such distinctions are not qualitative, therefore, but ones merely of order or timing; we move by due sequence, unforced and without inhibition, to a belief in what imagination has 'realized'.

[2] Alexander Pope, *Elegy to the memory of an unfortunate lady*, ll. 17–20.
[3] *BL*, chap. xiv, p. 152.

How 'imagination' may be distinguished from 'reason' and 'feeling' is best understood if we see how it informs the life of one whose authority derives from his being at once a philosopher of imagination and a successful practitioner. I refer to the author of both the *Biographia Literaria* and *The Ancient Mariner*—Samuel Taylor Coleridge.

In December 1796, Coleridge moved from the neighbourhood of Bristol to Nether Stowey in the Quantock Hills of Somerset, 'and devoted my thoughts and studies to the foundations of religion and morals'. He was joined by the poet William Wordsworth (first met in Bristol in the autumn of 1795) and his sister who had rented Alfoxden House in a neighbouring village. Here Coleridge wrote his major poetry (*The Ancient Mariner*, the first part of *Christabel*, and *Kubla Khan*). With Wordsworth he produced the *Lyrical Ballads* (1798) with the then revolutionary purpose of choosing 'incidents and situations from common life . . . and to throw over them a certain colouring of imagination, whereby ordinary things should be presented to the mind in an unusual aspect'.

A year before Schleiermacher published his *On Religion, Speeches addressed to its cultured despisers*, rebuking the English for their 'miserable empiricism', Coleridge and Wordsworth had published a challenge to those negative philosophers who call 'the want of imagination Judgement, and the never being moved to rapture Philosophy'. Imprisoned within utopian rationalism, Wordsworth had hoped from the French Revolution what it could not provide. Coleridge showed him how the imaginative life of man is linked with the life of God through the experience of Nature, and how the mind, far from being a machine, is like an 'instrument of few strings yet vast compass, played on by a musician of Genius'. Wordsworth has been called Coleridge's masterpiece. He certainly gave Coleridge back his thoughts in poetry of classic simplicity:

> Sweet is the lore which Nature brings;
> Our meddling intellect
> Mis-shapes the beauteous forms of things:—
> We murder to dissect.

Coleridge also enabled him to write 'the first great philosophical poem' in English, *The Prelude*, which expresses how his imaginative powers were impaired and then restored. The wider implications of Coleridge's thought are that poetry, far from being misrepresentation, as Bentham, Hume, and their fellow empiricists asserted, was the fullest and most fundamental use of language, being 'the best words in the best order'. Thus when religious assertions (particularly in Scripture) are linguistically and formally similar to poetic or imaginative assertions, they become 'the living educts of the imagination, . . . consubstantial with the truths of which they are the conductors'.

Coleridge distinguishes imagination—'the living power and prime agent' of perception—from fancy (the mere association of ideas in allegories and similes). He further distinguishes primary from secondary imagination, where the latter (literary or 'human' imagination) is the 'echo' of the former (God's 'eternal act of creation'). The literary imagination 'dissolves, diffuses, dissipates in order to re-create', and by thus providing a new unity to our perceptions, it extends our consciousness. Epistemologically, the consequences are that since 'the mind be not passive, if it be indeed made in God's image . . . any system built upon the passiveness of the mind must be false, as a system'. It may be objected that Coleridge's conception of imagination, in general, and of language as used in poetry, in particular, is unduly theological in origin. It is certainly so in its consequences. When, for example, he criticizes Wordsworth for taking too external and partial a view of language in his preference for the language of 'low and rustic life' in the preface to the *Lyrical Ballads*, Coleridge does so by reference to a '*lingua communis*', which exists everywhere in parts, and nowhere as a whole.[4] This implies that the language of poetry, politics, and religion can be understood and verified only within the community which uses it; and yet it also implies that such language 'is the armoury of the human mind; and at once contains the trophies of its past, and the weapons of its future conquests'.[5]

It is from this standpoint that Coleridge conducts a much wider criticism—that of the prevailing rationalism, and of its mechanistic and univocal theories of language. He goes behind

[4] *BL*, p. 173.
[5] *BL*, p. 159.

Hobbes, Descartes, and Bacon by speaking as if metaphor is primary, and plain, literal, meanings are a secondary, derived, and abstracted mode of language. 'And as every passion has its proper pulse, so will it likewise have its characteristic modes of expression.'[6] Each universe of discourse has, as it were, an appropriate range; and the language in its totality—the *lingua communis*–must be treated as hermeneutic or world-revealing.

Words, therefore, are more than mere counters of social intercourse, 'they are living powers, by which the things of most importance to mankind are actuated, combined, and humanized'. It is the poets who safeguard the range of language—Shakespeare's achievement is the dominion, 'often domination' he exercises over the full range of the language, whilst giving to the single perfect word that feeling of reality which 'heats and burns, makes itself felt. If we do not grasp it, it seems to grasp us.'[7]

It is within language thus conceived that we grow as persons, and move to certitude. In *Aids to Reflection* Coleridge develops a conception of assent or commitment which is to be found implicitly in Wordsworth's *Prelude* and explicitly in Newman's *Grammar of Assent*. Its roots probably lie in Butler and Berkeley; and it rests on the assumption that 'to believe and to understand are not diverse things, but the same thing in different periods of growth'.[8] Such a distinction helps us to grasp how a peasant may legitimately hold a belief he cannot explain, or how an agnostic, who cannot profess a belief, may be said to have faith—however unconscious or inhibited his predisposition may be. Faith and belief, too, are terms for the same thing in different stages of its growth. Almost, but not synonymous, they can appear as distinct from each other as the child is from the man, or the acorn from the oak.

This growth is both linguistic and social: knowledge grows in the act of using or adapting language to new experience, since 'the powers of conscious intellect increase by the accession of an organon or new word'.[9] The consequences of this view are elucidated in the *Lay Sermons* and the *Constitution of the Church and*

[6] *BL*, p. 184.
[7] *BL*, 157; *Aids to Reflection*, p. xix.
[8] *Aids to Reflection* (1825), London, Bohn, 1904, p. 128.
[9] *CN* 3268, Feb. 1808.

State, where Coleridge is clearly presupposing that the linguistic community is not the nation merely, but the nation as expressive of the Church (to which he gives the term 'Enclesia').

It is when we turn to Coleridge's *Notebooks* that we can see, not only how he uses the term 'imagination', but how, by a succession of imaginative acts, he fashions many of his celebrated maxims from diverse reflections on magnetism, galvanism, chemistry, and medicine, as well as from writers as diverse as the Schoolmen and Schiller. The charge of plagiarism (still repeated) overlooks this assimilating and re-creating power, which it was Coleridge's distinction to define and exemplify.

Such views also preserved Coleridge from believing that the existence of God could be demonstrated or empirically verified by evidence or other forms of the 'mechanical understanding'. For him (as Newman noted) God's existence was a moral (not a mathematical) certainty—'passions (or feelings) converging into the sensation of Positiveness'. Noting the distinction between certainly knowing and clearly knowing, he was as strongly convinced as von Hügel that the most dangerous threat to religion was to yield to 'the pleasure from clear and distinct notions', since the quintessential characteristic of religious language is of 'words that convey all their separate meanings at once, no matter how incomprehensible or absurd the *collective* meaning may be'; and to master such a language requires 'hard thinking and close self-energy'.[10]

Atheism, by contrast, is essentially a failure of imaginative *feeling*. Beginning in the alienation of the senses, it leads to the experience of oneself as living no longer as an inmate of this active universe, but in an 'empty echo-chamber or whispering labyrinth', where 'Coxcombs vanquish Berkeley with a grin'.

In revealing the origins and growth of Coleridge's triumph over those sufferings, which lasted from 1800 until 1816, and to describe which he coined the term 'psycho-somatic', the *Notebooks* also reveal the growing dependence for him of religion upon imagination. Although in outward appearance he grew increasingly disorderly and procrastinating, he retained both method and energy (he once walked 263 miles in 8 days to combat his drug addiction). But that energy—the 'close self-

[10] *CN* 3628.

energy' of the *Notebooks*—was directed not to what Schleier-macher had called the national preoccupation—'our all-sucking, all-whirling Money-Eddy', but to the enlargement of consciousness. This—an objective common to the poet and the psychotherapist—required him to realize that his method was the very reverse of the system-building required for a *magnum opus*. Instead it must aim to create a self-conscious imagination by meditating on experiences in the act of experiencing. Al-though he frequently speaks of his having been a Socinian, then almost a Pantheist, he never moved far from the Trinitarian orthodoxy he now espoused. What suffering forced him to do was to 'read the New Testament again'; and his *Notebooks* establish for the first time the extent to which his subsequently published thought arises from a growing power of religious feeling. Although he had urged against the Empiricists that 'in wonder all philosophy began: in wonder it ends', he had added, 'But the first wonder is the off-spring of ignorance; the last is the parent of adoration.'[11] Religion was also at the root of his distinction between wisdom and knowledge: 'When I worship, let me unify. . . . To be wise I must know all things as *one*; to be knowing I must perceive the absolutely indivisible as infinitely distinguishable.' His continual association of religion and poetry is especially significant, holding as he did that 'at times we should awake and step forward—and this is effected by poetry and religion. The Extenders of Consciouness—sorrow, sickness, poetry, and religion. The truth is, we stop in the sense of Life just when we are not *forced* to go on—and then adopt a permission of our feelings for a precept of our Reason.'[12]

It is difficult to disentangle the strands of Coleridge's criti-cism, which is simultaneously literary, social, and theological. This, the result of a deliberate intention, is the source, not of weakness, but of a continuing strength and relevance. Since he is as much concerned to preserve the dependence of imagina-tion upon religion, as that of religion upon imagination, his argument cuts both ways; but his criticism is, as I have said, also of continuing relevance. In the *Lay Sermon* he diagnoses the chief trouble of his own time as arising from 'the over-balance of the commercial spirit', or, as we might say, an unfettered

[11] *Aids to Reflection*, Aphorism IX, p. 156.
[12] *CN* 3632.

obsession with economic growth. The effect upon religion, then as now, is to divorce it from learning and imagination, by restricting it to an unreflecting pietism or illuminism.[13]

Theology, on the other hand, 'tends to defraud the student of his worldly wisdom . . . by pre-occupying his thoughts in the acquisition of knowledge'. Either religion must occupy the whole mind, 'being a total act of the soul', or it is not authentic; and as the poet 'brings the whole soul of man into activity', so must religion, which is both 'the poetry and philosophy of all mankind'. In other words, separate religion from scholarship and the arts, and it either evaporates or becomes the prisoner of practical men and of their needs.

The world which rejected this analysis becomes the world of the Dickens novels. It is that of the Gradgrinds, Bounderbys, Veneerings, and Pumblechooks—hard-nosed practical men, who aim to keep the distinction between persons and things as blurred as possible. They are with us still in the 'developers' of old, shabby, unproductive communities. But what Coleridge also saw was the extent to which the predominance of such men prevents the practice of a *sacramental* faith in either the secular or religious sense. This is surely what he is driving at when, in an oft-quoted passage from the first *Lay Sermon*, he contrasts the language of Scripture—'the living *educts* of the Imagination'— with the writing of his own time, 'the product of an unenlivened generalizing Understanding'—a perfect description of management English.[14]

13 'For the Religion of best repute among us holds all the truths of Scripture and all the doctrines of Christianity so very transcendent, or so very easy, as to make study or research either vain or needless . . . and thus habitually *taking for granted* all truths of spiritual import (it) leaves the understanding vacant and at leisure for a thorough insight into present and temporal interests: which, doubtless, is the true reason why its followers are in general, such shrewd, knowing, wary, well-informed, thrifty and thriving men of business.' *Lay Sermons*, ed. R. J. White, *Collected Works*, vol. vi, 1972, p. 194.

14 'A hunger-bitten and idea-less philosophy naturally produces a starveling and comfortless religion. It is among the miseries of the present age that it recognises no medium between *Literal* and *Metaphorical*. Faith is either to be buried in the dead letter, or its name and honours usurped by a counterfeit product of the mechanical understanding, which in the blindness of self-complacency confounds SYMBOLS with ALLEGORIES. Now an Allegory is but a translation of abstract notions into a picture-language, which is itself nothing but an abstraction from objects of the senses. . . . On the other hand a Symbol . . . always partakes of the Reality it renders intelligible; and while it enunciates the whole, abides itself as a living part in that Unity, of which it is the representative.' *The Statesman's Manual*, in *Lay Sermons*, p. 30.

If we fail, therefore, to concede a middle ground between hard fact and mere fantasy, we deny the possibility of a religious faith which is sacramental, because we deny transcendence to 'the incidents and situations of common life'. As well as sacraments, metaphors and symbols will be treated as mere allegories, and philosophers will dismiss an appeal to 'imagination' as a category mistake. Furthermore, poetic faith and religious belief will be regarded as representing two distinct and disassociated starting-points. Literary faith will be negatively conceived, in theory, as merely a suspension of disbelief, while religion, in practice, will become de-mythologized into notions, articles of belief, and legal precepts.

This returns us to the questions raised at the beginning. If this is the state of affairs which has occurred ought we not to conceive a great divide as having grown up between ourselves and an age of faith? Has the conception of metaphor, symbol, and sacrament Coleridge commends been superseded chronologically—that is by a unique and irreversible historical process of social and intellectual change?

(III) THE CHRONOLOGY OF METAPHOR

A 'great divide' is what is implied in a famous distinction made by T. S. Eliot between the Metaphysical poets of the seventeenth century and their successors. Eliot values the Metaphysicals for their ability, essential to poetry, to 'devour any kind of experience'. They were thus 'constantly amalgamating disparate experience'. Later poets did 'not feel their thought as immediately as the odour of a rose'. To Donne, however, 'a thought . . . was an experience; it modified his sensibility'. In later poets, such a sensibility becomes 'dissociated': thought and feeling become separate activities.[15] This is evident in the writing of Milton, whose poetry can be read either 'solely for the sound' or 'for the sense', and not as in Shakespeare or Dante, where 'at each reading all the elements of appreciation can be present'.[16]

The distinctions made by Eliot between the Metaphysicals and the later poets are no longer accepted by students of literature (particularly the suggestion that Milton was somehow

---

[15] *SE* (1969), pp. 287–8.
[16] *OPP*, p. 143.

'responsible' for such changes); and Eliot himself later admitted that the causes of such 'dissociation of sensibility' went much deeper than the innovating tendencies of a particular poet, however great, perverse, or original his genius.[17]

Even so, the problem remains. It requires us to think in terms of a change of consciousness as between our age and another, in which the preferred age is past, yet richer. As Eliot came to see, this is not a merely literary problem; and I would suggest that it is best to see it as one common to literature and theology, since, in each case, attention seems to be focused on the Caroline divines, or on those whom I would prefer to regard as the survivors of Renascence Humanism.

It is Coleridge, rather than Eliot, who sees this overlap most fruitfully. For him, it is the polemical theological controversies which come to a head in the Civil War that are responible for the destruction of sensibility Eliot prescribes. While Behmen, George Fox, and William Law 'kept alive the heart in the head',[18] it is the polemical and 'systematic theology' of the 'anti-Prelatic divines, whether Episcopalians or Presbyterians', which 'quenched all fineness of mind, all flow of heart, all grandeur of imagination'. Speaking of the party which had been 'victorious' over Richard Baxter, Coleridge writes:

the Prelatic Arminians, enriched as they were with all learning and highly gifted with taste and judgement, had emptied revelation of all the doctrines that can properly be said to have been revealed, and thus equally caused the extinction of the imagination, and quenched the life in the light by withholding the appropriate fuel and the supporters of the sacred flame. So that, between both parties, our transcendent liturgy remains like an ancient Greek temple, a monumetal proof of the architectural genius of an age long departed, when there were giants in the land.[19]

We are confronted by a change of sensibility, therefore, which is not confined to poetry, but has both a literary and a theological form. It is an overlap which can only be most profitaby elucidated if it is examined from each point of view respectively. The *theological* form of the question is what are the primary forms of religious belief? Are they the metaphors and

[17] In 1947: see *OPP*, pp. 152–61 *passim*.
[18] *BL*, chap. ix, p. 70.
[19] *Lit. Rem.* iv. 119.

symbols from which the Caroline divines started, and which they took for granted; or was Dr Johnson right in believing (along with the later seventeenth- and eighteenth-century rational theologians) that the work of theology was properly that of de-mythologizing such metaphors into 'truths'?[20]

Conversely, in the poetry of Donne and Herbert, literary adequacy seems to denote a religious adequacy, and vice versa. Its adequacy is manifested in a particular *density* of metaphor; and it is this which pre-eminently characterizes the poetry of the Shakespearean tragedies. It is a density at once literary and religious. Are its occurrence and coincidence accidents of time and circumstance, merely? Has this use of metaphor a chronology, so that attempts to realize it anew (as in *Four Quartets*) are merely attempts to put the clock back, to seek a simple 'homecoming' behind the Industrial Revolution, or whatever divide we choose to mark the unique change of consciousness between ourselves and the seventeenth century?

Today, theologians might be prepared to acquiesce in such a view; but literary critics continue to assert that in Shakespeare the resources of the language are most fully realized. Is there then a theological equivalent? Is there a peculiar authenticity in a religious language so metaphorically 'dense' as to be resistant to theological 'reduction'? Some religious assertions of a primary kind do indeed seem linguistically similar to poetic assertions. How else are we to respond to the claim in scripture that Christ is both shepherd and lamb? His teaching in the parables, for example, on the good shepherd[21] or on the kingdom of heaven [22] can be understood only as we engage with the metaphors and with their interaction; the kingdom is both a seed, a leaven, a pearl, and a treasure.[23]

This exposes an important distinction, philosophically. It is between understanding what is said, because we can say it in another way equally well by putting it 'in our own words'; and understanding what is said because these words are in these positions, and the right words are in the right order.[24] This is the distinction which Coleridge pins down in his definition of

[20] See below, p. 116.
[21] John 10.
[22] Matt. 13:52.
[23] See below, Part Three pp. 000ff.
[24] Wittgenstein's distinction in *Philosophical Investigations*, Oxford, 1953, para. 531.

poetry as the best words in the best order, [25] since what makes
poetry great is the degree of its resistance (or opacity) to paraphrase. It cannot without loss be translated into other words: it
is thus an *uninvertible* use of language, whose meaning cannot be
separated from its form, whereas prose is a use of language
which is convertible or *reducible*.

When Macbeth, for example, is deciding whether he will kill
his guest, Duncan, he describes the consequences thus:

> And Pity, like a naked new-born babe,
> Striding the blast, or Heaven's cherubin, hors'd
> Upon the sightless couriers of the air,
> Shall blow the horrid deed in every eye,
> That tears shall drown the wind. I have no spur
> To prick the sides of my intent, but only
> Vaulting ambition, which o'er leaps itself
> And falls on the other. (I. vii. 20)

Although we speak of this language as richly metaphorical,
and know what it says, we cannot easily explain how it gains its
effects, since its metaphors are so mixed as to be—in a strictly
logical sense—contradictory, even nonsensical. How can new-
born babes stride the blast, what is a sightless courier of the air,
other than the air itself, and if vaulting ambition is a spur, how
can it o'erleap itself? How does one know that these are the
wrong questions to put? To look for a chain of connected
inferences or deductions would be to gain a series of almost
identical paraphrases. The momentum is not logical, but analogical: metaphors accumulate and in accumulating modify
each other. It is like the difference between the stills which make
up the film, and the film itself: each shift in the metaphor must
be taken, not as complete in itself, but as it relates to the whole
context. To stop and weigh each word (testing it for contradiction) before we go to the next is proper only to the second
stage of our response: initially we must take a deep breath and
read the poem 'with our ears'. We must notice that certain
words, by virtue of their position rhythmically, bear a special
indicating stress, and that this tells us how to read it, and
therefore how to order our response: *pity . . . striding* the blast.

---

[25] In *Table Talk*, Oxford, 1917, p. 73. *Shakespearean Criticism*, ed. T. M. Raysor,
London, Everyman edn., 1960, i. 148, ii. 42.

Heaven's cherubin . . . shall *blow* the horrid deed in every eye. Our response to these words in these positions is also one to that facility in metaphor which Aristotle held to be the distinguishing characteristic of a poet. This facility is, as Coleridge remarks, to 'hover between images', so that we never settle into a mere image, and are always prevented from saying 'It only means ——', or 'it means nothing more than ——'.

In the passage quoted, the words do not stand for terms possessing a constant meaning, but rather for constituents of a magnetic field, their signification being that of the field as a whole. In this case it is the complete play. As with the other great tragedies, it acts therefore as an extended metaphor. For example, the image of the babe is linked to the milk of human kindness later in the play; and the image of vaulting ambition is yet another of those inter-related images of frustration, which themselves relate to those of 'equivocation', the experience of which is at the heart of the protagonist's experience. We do not properly understand what Shakespeare intends to signify until he has finished: as a philosopher has remarked in speaking of religious language, we have to wait for the penny to drop, since here is evidence of a mind that has possessed in a unified apprehension all that it wants to say before composition: it is the view as a *whole*. For Schleiermacher this was the characteristic common to both religion and music.[26] This is true of Mozart, but it is also true of Shakespeare and Wordsworth—what they wanted to say was there before they started: composition was merely committing the unity to paper.

Not only is it possible that an apprehension at once so rich and varied yet so unified can be expressed only in the manner I have described, it is historically indisputable that such a use of language is easier when, as in Elizabethan times, the meanings of the words are in flux and the language is in growth. Shakespeare's language is that of an active not of a reflective people—to see is to act—and it is nearer the condition of primitive society, where the meaning of a word is learnt not through reflection but through use. In order to understand the meanings of terms, even the concept of rationality, especially in such societies, we must understand their way of life, not superimpose

---

[26] *On Religion, Speeches addressed to its cultured despisers* 1893, p. 51. Cp. his remark 'What the word makes clear, music must make *alive.*'

upon it our own, with its highly generalized concepts: if, as one historian remarks, it is difficult to be chivalrous without a horse, it may be equally difficult to understand 'honour' if we no longer bear swords.

Shakespeare's language, that also of the Authorized version of the Bible, is akin to the Hebraic, in that it is the language of a small community, of feeling and action. It is fully explicit *morally*: it appears to repeat itself, to stand still: it is tenacious of the truth it has, rather than concerned to discover a new truth. It explains and enforces. The objects and events of daily life manifest a transcendent, divine order. This, the social, temporal world, thus partakes of the divine order it renders intelligible and signifies: it is 'sacramental' of it, in the same manner as its 'values' are explicitly located within a 'sacramental' conception of value in general. Thus the King's murder in Macbeth is literally 'sacrilegious':

> Most sacrilegious murder hath broke ope
> The Lord's anointed temple, and stole thence
> The life o' the building! (II. iii. 50)

St. Paul's manner of describing the Church is similar. Confused or mixed metaphors occur, but their logic is disregarded, since they refer to a common referent, whose reality is never in question: 'the metaphors themselves are the secondary deductions from the primal communal experience.'[27] Thus Paul can speak of the body in terms of mixed metaphors drawn from building, planting, nation, and table, [28] while John can visualize the bride as a city, temple, mother, virgin, and choir.[29]

This culture was so close in form and spirit to the Hebraic that not only did it produce a truly vernacular bible, but—at the hands of Cranmer—a vernacular liturgy. These, by making so convincingly explicit what was implicit in contemporary culture and sensibility, succeeded in becoming the sources of its authentication.

Thus, in *Macbeth*, evil is so intensely felt, because both writer and audience experience it as objectively 'real'. What religion

---

[27] Paul S. Minnear, *Images of the Church in the New Testament*, London, 1961, pp. 252, 224–5.
[28] 1 Cor. 3:9.
[29] Rev. 21:2.

promises, reality proves. 'The wages of sin is death.' To the sinner, life becomes 'a tale told by an idiot, full of sound and fury, signifying nothing'. These are not pragmatic fictions entertained by a willing suspension of disbelief. They are analogues; and Shakespeare's art is in showing not whether they are so, but *how* they are so.

The method of the poets is that also of the preachers. Lancelot Andrewes crumbles the text, in order to elicit analogies (by detecting resemblances). Thus in his Sermon on the coming of the Holy Ghost (Luke 4:18–19),[30] Andrewes speaks of it as an anointing of Christ's head, and moves quickly to speak of our being anointed by books:

> On his head the whole boxe of ointment was broken, which from Him ran down upon the Apostles, somewhat more fresh and full; and (ever) the further, the thinner, as the nature of things liquid is: but, some small streames trickle down even to us, and to our times still. . . . I shall not need tell you, the Spirit comes not upon us now at our conception in the womb, to anoint us there. No: we behoove to light our lamps oft, and to spend much oyle at our studies, ere we can atteine it. This way, come we to our anointing now, by bookes; this Booke chiefly, but in a good part also, by the bookes of the Ancient Fathers, and Lights of the Church, in whom the scent of this ointment was fresh, and the temper true; on whose writings it lieth thick, and we thence strike it off and gather it safely.

As well as being the method of the Ancient Fathers, it is that of the earliest Christian speech—'occasional' rather than studied; oral rather than written, [31] it is a thinking by accumulation, not progression; and, as T. S. Eliot remarks, 'his emotion grows as he moves more deeply into his subject'.[32] This Andrewes does by 'iterating', that is, by 'hitting the point and hitting it again. . . . He is never tired of using the same word: it meets us again and again in every shape and connexion, and pierces and perforates the whole sermon.'[33] In this way, a

[30] Lancelot Andrewes, *Ninety-Six Sermons*, Oxford, 1841, iii. 291.

[31] As Matthew Arnold noted (see below, p. 99); see Amos N. Wilder, *Early Christian Rhetoric*, London, 1964, p. 20.

[32] *SE*, p. 351. Eliot's critique derives expressly from F. E. Brightman's Introduction to his edition of Andrewes's *Preces Privatae* (1903). Eliot does not seem to have realized that this, in turn, is derived from J. B. Mozley's analysis published in *The British Critic* as 'Bishop Andrewes' Sermons' (vol. xxxi, no. 61, Jan. 1842, pp. 167–205).

[33] *M.*, p. 193.

particularly striking climax is gained in such typical phrases as 'Christ is no wild cat, what think ye of twelve days', or 'the word within a word unable to speak a word'. Thus 'a single word reminds the hearer not only of that word as it stood by itself, but of the portion of the text whence it came', as Mozley remarks.[34] And we are again reminded of Shakespeare's similar use of metaphors, which gain their significance by their placing within the play as a whole.

Because the function of the sermon is both to 'explain and enforce',[35] Eliot is justified in speaking of Andrewes's method as 'terminating in the ecstasy of assent'.[36] In its own way, it is systematic: its quickness, dexterity, and richness enable his theological explanations to 'show the connexion of one great doctrine with another, the bearings of one great fact of Christianity upon another, with admirable decision and completeness'.[37] It is a further example of the method to be discussed later,[38] by which religious 'figures' or analogues are modified: each corrects the sense of the other: we say and unsay to a positive result:

> Set this down then; Christianity is a meeting . . . a cross meeting of four virtues that seem to be in a kind of opposition . . . and to this meeting there go *pia dogmata* as well as *bona opera*—Righteousness as well as Truth. Err not this error then, to single any out as it were in disgrace of the rest; say not, one will serve the turn,—what should we do with the rest of the four? Take not a figure, and make of it a plain speech; seek not to be saved by Synedoche. Each of these is a quarter of Christianity, you shall never while you live make it serve for the whole. The truth is,—sever them, and farewell all.[39]

Here is a method, the very opposite of that used later for discovering radically new intepretations or metaphysical explanations. The later method requires, as its condition of operation, a total suspension of belief, and a standpoint wholly external to what is being investigated. Such was the method of the men who came after—Swift and the Augustan satirists, Hume and Bentham.

[34] *M.*, p. 175.
[35] *M.*, p. 176.
[36] *SE*, p. 347.
[37] *M.*, p. 173.
[38] See below, p. 63.
[39] *Of the Nativity*, Christmas Day, 1616 (*Ninety-Six Sermons*, Oxford, 1841, i. 192–3).

As Eliot points out, Andrewes's method is Newman's. It is so indeed, as Mozley's appreciation in the *British Critic* makes clear. This was written in 1842, when Newman's influence on Mozley was at its height and the Oxford Movement moving towards its climax. Dean Church specifically makes the comparison in his sermon on Bishop Andrewes (1877). What is significant is that this method—so akin to the accumulation of probabilities which converge powerfully and concurrently to precipitate a real assent—is also Eliot's in *Four Quartets*.

Its opposite is what, nowadays, might be called a free expressiveness which, Mozley notes, so often reveals 'a dreamy clouded philosophy, a sentimental tone of feeling, and a weak, diffuse, and diluted style'.[40] Coleridge is sharper still, when he writes of 'an unenlivened, generalising Understanding'.[41] By contrast, Andrewes is commended in terms recalling Wordsworth's definition of poetry, for his 'spontaneous overflowings of feeling'.

By such means, by the accumulation of analogies, the order of the Universe or the moral law is *apprehended* as distinct from being *comprehended*. That is to say, we believe in or grasp *how* it is, rather than understand *why* it is so; but by such belief we gain what comprehension we can. Thus, although Macbeth has, by his sins, lost what Dante calls the good of the intellect, namely that clarity of moral insight which is the opposite of 'equivocation', he comes to understand what he has never ceased to believe: that his vaulting ambition has cost him 'honour, love, obedience, troops of friends'; and that Duncan's virtues have pleaded successfully 'trumpet-tongued against the deep damnation of his taking-off'.

Both in its positive and negative aspects this is the sensibility which Eliot terms 'associated', one in which both feeling and thought are immediately at one.

Its expression is complex, not reductive. Thus Dante, in commending his *Divine Comedy*, writes: 'The sense of this work is not simple, but on the contrary it may be called polysemous, that is to say, "of more senses than one".'[42] He distinguishes what is to be understood literally, from what is allegorically

---

[40] *M.*, p. 203.
[41] See above, p. 14.
[42] Letter to Can Grande', *Epistolae* X, E.T. London, Temple Classics, 1904, p. 347.

intended (itself composed of three distinguishable layers or senses). Such density of metaphorical allusion can cope with what is ambiguous and paradoxical in human experience, without attempting to reduce the questions to answers. It shows and suffers the polarities eikonographically, in, for example, the conflict of good and evil, Satan and God, whilst assuming their ultimate resolution.[43] Its achievement invites such descriptions as 'poise' or 'irony', consisting, as it does, of the ability to 'amalgamate disparate experiences', or to be aware of experiences other than those which are directly stated.

The form of its expression is essentially poetic (whether it be a sermon or a play); but when it is held that there is always a better way of saying what the poet says, when his metaphors are held to be inferior to clear and distinct conceptions, or when reason is elevated above feeling, we are close to the dissociation of sensibility.

Coleridge's dating of this shift or dissociation as occurring around 1688 is correct, as may be seen if, as he does, we compare preaching styles.[44] When Tillotson died in 1694, it was said of his preaching 'that he said what was just necessary to give clear ideas of things and no more'. What Coleridge calls 'the transfer of interest' may be gauged if we compare this with Andrewes or Donne (of whom it was said that he 'wrought' upon the understanding and affections).

The characteristic density of metaphor I have been describing does not, with certain exceptions, extend into the eighteenth and nineteenth centuries; but it is also necesary to conceive the matter chronologically, because in speaking of metaphor now we are obliged to distinguish at least two kinds of use. I refer to a second (though not necessarily later) use of metaphor which can be detected even in the last plays of Shakespeare. It is usual to speak of the symbolic references in these plays as being in some ways more explicit or deliberate than in the tragedies. We slip into talking about common themes, such as reconciliation or the restoration of a lost royalty. When, in the *Winter's Tale*, Hermione accepts the unjust sentence by saying 'this action I now go on is for my better grace', we notice that references to 'grace' and 'blood' in this play work in a different way from

[43] Erich Auerbach, *Mimesis*, Princeton, 1968, p. 555.
[44] In *Lay Sermons*, pp. 197f.

those to 'light' and 'dark' in *Macbeth*, for example. We feel a
pressure to interpret, to paraphrase, to interchange their meaning with another: so much in the structure of the last plays
seems to stand for a meaning expressible in other, perhaps more
specifically theological, terms.

But it is in the nineteenth century and in the poetry of
Matthew Arnold that we become most aware of what may be
called this second use of metaphor. His scholar gipsy,

> '-twirling in thy hand a withered spray,
> And waiting for the spark from heaven to fall . . .

> Still nursing the unconquerable hope,
> Still clutching the inviolable shade,

immune from 'this strange disease of modern life', provokes us
into asking what he stands for, into looking for a further significance, and into asking what the poet *means* or *intends*. Likewise
Arnold's references in '*Dover Beach*' to the 'sea of faith', to the
'darkling plain . . . where ignorant armies clash by night', or in
Grande Chartreuse to our being between two worlds are of a kind
that seem to invite us to inquire further. I would call this use of
metaphor *translucent* (as distinct from opaque or *dense*), because
it seems to refer to thoughts and ideas which we must first
comprehend in order to apprehend. In other words, it seems to
invite, even demand, interpretation or paraphrase.

Although, the same point might be made about understanding Shakespeare's use of 'pity' in *Macbeth*, to understand 'pity'
seems different from understanding 'the sea of faith', 'the
strange disease of modern life', or even the terms 'blood' and
'grace' in the *Winter's Tale*. 'Pity' is intended as a self-evident
reference; and the metaphorical expansion which is the play
provides the context for its use and therefore for its further
understanding. Thus, when Macbeth suffers the effects of denying pity, and of obeying 'vaulting ambition' in Act V (iii,
22–28), the simple, even trite description of what he has for-
feited—'honour, love, obedience, troops of friends'—acquires
an increasingly terrifying force as the context widens from the
immediate 'My life has fall'n into the sear, the yellow leaf', to
darker, larger metaphors of perverted nature and equivocation
which form the crucible of the play.

Similarly, in *Lear* (V. ii. 9), the metaphor 'ripeness is all' strikes us as leading to the heart of the play because of all the other metaphors in which its use and meaning are set—to those of endurance, to being bound upon a wheel of fire, and to those which show how we are all 'foolish, fond, old men'. Such use of metaphor does not demand interpretation or completion, but brings powerfully alive a sense of order, unity, or organism apparently in terms of what it is itself. It creates or expresses a world, it does not point out of itself to another order of situations of which it is the allegory. Is it then expressive of an order which is self-enclosed and autonomous? Or is it not the metaphor which appears self-sufficient but the referent to which it points and so fully realizes? A further point of contrast is that such uses of metaphor seem to have a performative emphasis: pity and ripeness are understood as they are acted out and in terms of the dramatic action, from which our comprehension must not be separated: what they really are takes the story to tell. In this they seem akin to what Berkeley in *Alciphron* calls operative principles, which serve to regulate conduct, and whose under-standing is completed only as they are performed.

The second use of metaphor is, as I have said, less resistant to paraphrase, seeming to depend upon what is already explicit, or to require it to be made so. Such metaphors illustrate rather than discover, and although they may 'suspend' our disbelief, what they refer to is not as self-evidently real as that which the metaphors of Shakespeare and Andrewes render intelligible. We choose to 'put on' the scholar gipsy's 'hat of antique shape, and cloak of grey', or choose to see ourselves as if we were upon a darkling plain, twirling withered sprays gathered from the stony rubbish of the waste land, unwatered by the sea of faith. In Arnold's own words (used mistakenly of biblical metaphor) it is 'language *thrown out* at an object of consciousness not fully grasped, which inspired emotion'.[45] It seems to be a use of metaphor for states of mind which are in some way *imaginatively* incomplete, as if the poet had suffered the reductive pressure of rationality so intensely that his metaphors seek completion in some more reflective mode of discourse, and cannot be convinc-ingly apprehended, until they have *first* been successfully ex-plained or authenticated. For example, with the entry of the

[45] *Literature and Dogma*, London, 1891, p. 30.

Tyrian trader at the conclusion of *The Scholar-Gipsy*, the metaphor collapses into versified theory. Was it this use of metaphor that Keats had in mind, when he said that poetry is not so fine a thing as philosophy, because an eagle is not so fine a thing as truth?

By contrast with that of *Macbeth*, Arnold's poetry lacks that substantiality, that sense of imaginative re-creation and completion: these words do not have to be unconditionally in these positions. What the author expresses seems to have been already present to him in another mode *before* its expression in the poetry; and in saying this one is reminded of Dr Johnson's strictures upon religious poetry.[46] Coleridge quotes an amusing example of a more extreme instance still—of the ingenious gentleman under the influence of the tragic muse: the greeting, '"I wish you a good morning sir." "Thank you, sir, and I wish you the same"', became:

> To you a morning good, good sir, I wish.
> You sir! I thank: to you the same wish I.

The first use of metaphor certainly requires us to elucidate its meaning and intention—if we are to read it intelligently—but what it *signifies* is created in the successful juxtaposing, interacting, and yoking of its images. This is what creates the metaphor and leads us to say that what a metaphor tells us is itself. The wonder is (to paraphrase Wittgenstein) not in what the words mean, but in our being moved by what we cannot explain in other terms.

It is precisely this uninvertible, irreducible character of the first use of metaphor which is that also of the primary, or rudimentary, forms of religious faith. Such statements as 'the taking of manhood into God' have, as Newman reminds us, either a very abject or human meaning, or none at all. There is, he says 'no inward view' of these doctrines, because the metaphors by which they are signified 'are not mere symbols of ideas which exist independently of them, but their meaning is coincident and identical with the ideas'.[47] In other words, there are no further expressions for which these are the expression. To

[46] See below, p. 116.

[47] *OUS*, p. 338. Newman goes on to warn us against such conceptions, however, if they lead us to conclude that we can have 'no true idea of Almighty God, but only an earthly one'.

learn how to respond to such metaphors is not so much to understand why God exists but how he exists, since they do not tell us what God is, or what the taking of manhood into God is, but how we should respond to it. It has a performative as well as an informative intention. As with Shakespeare's use of 'pity' in *Macbeth*, we learn not what pity is or the grounds for believing in its existence, but what its existence involves and how we should respond—how we should act in relation to its assertion.

To understand how metaphor works in what I have called the primary sense is also to understand how religious analogues work, and for what purpose. To take the passage from Job 3, used by Hardy to provide the tragic climax of *Jude the Obscure*,[48] is to see how analogical descriptions are used in scripture. Their effect is achieved by accumulation and convergence, rather than by inference and logical sequence; they hover between images, rather than settle into a dominant image:

(11) 'Why died I not from the womb? Why did I not give up the ghost when I came out of the belly? . . . (13) For now should I have lain still and been quiet. I should have slept: then had I been at rest!'

(20) 'Wherefore is light given to him that is in misery, and life unto the bitter in soul? . . . (23) Why is light given to a man whose way is hid, and whom God hath hedged in?'

We are not responding to a series of inferences from defined concepts, but to a rapid flow of images, which never settle into a mere finite definition; instead we become aware of the form of the language, of these words being in these positions, and of our need to attend to the *order* of what is said. Thus Coleridge, in commenting on John 3:6—'that which is born of the flesh, is flesh; that which is born of the spirit, is spirit'—notes that the order or form of the words in the first part of the verse is paralleled in the second part and gives, thereby, the procedure for making the second part intelligible.[49] Thus the rules for understanding the familiar term ('flesh') are the means by which the unfamiliar fact ('spirit') asserted in the second half of

[48] See below, p. 108.

[49] *Aids to Reflection*, p. 136. Cp. Newman's remark on the *form* of the descriptions of the Last Supper both in scripture and the Prayer Book: 'What *is* remarkable is the repeated mention of the very same acts in the same order—taking, blessing or giving thanks, and breaking.' *DA*, p. 180.

the expression is rendered intelligible; and analogical transformation occurs when the special characteristic of the second
term ('spirit') imposes its own rules upon the expression, thus
'spirit is like flesh, but is not like'. When this 'analogical leap',
as it is termed, has been successfully made, it informs our
discovery of what it is to be born again in the spirit: we have
discovered the source in the thing. For example, when Paul
talks of Christ's relation to his Church in terms of marriage, it is
as if, by placing ourselves in the married relationship, 'in some
secret way' we become aware of 'the divine relation of which it is
a figure'.[50] But analogy also expresses an essential ambiguity,
since its terms are simultaneously 'the same as' and 'different
from'. In the more formal words of the Fourth Lateran Council
of 1215, God and Creation are like one another, and yet even in
this resemblance completely unlike; and in every similarity,
however great, the dissimilarity is greater.[51] The heart-
piercing, reason-bewildering fact is that we apprehend our
separateness from God in our likeness to him.[52] In the same
manner such parables or stories as those of Job, or of Abraham
and Isaac work analogically by showing how our understanding is determined and limited by God's action towards us: God
does not deal with us, as we are obliged to deal with each other.
It is the understanding of this which prompts Kierkegaard to
speak of the 'suspension of the ethical' when he considers the
implications of the Abraham and Isaac story in *Fear and
Trembling*.

Some modern philosophers would go further. Ricoeur[53]
argues that the successful use of analogy in such stories, and
particularly in that of the Fall of Man, effects a 'transcendental
deduction' in the Kantian sense, if its use has been 'a means of
detecting and deciphering human reality, (since) it will have
been verified by its power to raise up, to illuminate, and *to give
order* to' the particular area of human experience, in this
instance that of evil. This is not so very different from
Newman's saying that revelation commits supernatural truths
'irrevocably' to language, since this, 'the dogmatic principle',

[50] Newman, *ECH* i. 43.

[51] Denzinger, *Enchiridion Symbolorum*, 1947, p. 432. When, in comparisons, the emphasis falls upon what is *dis*similar, the terms 'analogy' and 'analogue' are used.

[52] *Apo.*, p. 335.

[53] Paul Ricoeur, *The Symbolism of Evil*, Boston, 1969, p. 355 (my italics).

commits words to express 'new ideas' and therefore to 'a sacra-mental office'.[54]

Similarly, a contemporary theologian, F. W. Dillistone, in his treatment of atonement,[55] approaches it not as a 'doctrine' coherently conceived, and systematically developed, but as a developing series of analogues and parables, beginning with the pre-Christian analogue of universal regeneration through a central cosmic sacrifice. So wide-ranging an account of our sense of estrangement and reconciliation depends upon its origins in a pre-scientific world-view. With the growth of science such cosmic self-confidence begins to wane, although it is still evident in such analogues or parables as the juridical or penal one of the decisive judgement, and that of a unique redemption wrought by a single and decisive battle. In spite of their evident theoretical shortcomings such analogues and parables remain potent facts of the imagination, as in the case of *Paradise Lost*. Even when they cease to be readily available to us and lose theological, but not imaginative, plausibility, we must still live through them into our own analogues and parables. Thus we can continue to respond to Christ as the tragic hero, provided we realize that this parable is no more final than that of Christus Victor: if the latter implies a dualism which is finally unacceptable, the former can make of Christ's ultimate recon-ciliation nothing more than a paradox which is open to the kind of imaginative 'reduction' given to it by D. H. Lawrence in *The Man who Died*. Yet to say that there is more to the analogue 'atonement' than tragedy or victory is not to repudiate the analogues and parables that make up the history of its use; instead we must grow through them, accepting their correction to interpretations that more exactly fit our circumstances. They remain permanent possibilities of experience.

The question is whether the distinction I have been propos-ing between the two uses of metaphor points to a more general distinction between a first-order and a second-order use of language. What is first order is the successful use of forms of language as metaphors and analogues; and what is second order is their use *merely* as illustrations, interpretations, or pro-

<hr />

[54] *Dev.*, p. 303; cp. Coleridge in the passage cited above, p. 14.

[55] F. W., Dillistone, *The Christian understanding of Atonement*, London, 1968. This, a major contribution to the theological method here recommended, deserves close study. See also my review in *New Blackfriars*, vol. 50, no. 586, Mar. 1969, pp. 331–3.

jections (in Marx's sense). Such a distinction may suggest an even more fundamental one between the language of faith and the language of belief. What we must guard against initially is confusing first- and second-order usages by assuming that metaphors used analogically and symbolically are reducible wholly to clearly defined explanations or unambiguous forms of belief. Instead, their function is to hold a range of meanings in unity, and to keep them perpetually open to fresh interpretations. Thus our understanding of 'atonement' (or, conversely, of 'alienation') is comprised of all the metaphors and analogues we have assimilated. The modes of their operation—spoken of as a hovering between images, a saying and unsaying, a reconciling of paradox or contrasting modes, a propounding of verbal contradictions and ambiguities—are all terms for a breaking up or unsettling of usage, or of any determination to fix the sense conceptually. This use of metaphor to keep the sense broken and in growth, helps the poet to 'dislocate the languge into meaning'. When a metaphor meets a need of language and becomes a concept to be understood literally, it ceases to be a metaphor (e.g. the fate of words like 'gas', 'wireless', and 'cinema'). A problem for religion is when analogues and metaphors are wrongly held to have ceased to be so and are taken literally and conceptually. Perpetual vigilance needs to be exercised to keep such truths freed from 'verbal invasion', or from becoming clichés.

Although this may be true of many of the Dominical sayings in scripture and of the parables, what are we to make of Paul's development of the classical image of the body in 1 Corinthians 12, or his way of leading up to the assertion that we are members one of another in Ephesians 4:25? Are these examples of the first or second use of metaphor? And what of the articles of the Creed? Would we accept George Tyrrell's assertion that 'I do not feel bound to find *how* each bit of the creed helps to the one truth symbolised by the whole'?[56]

[56] 'I will not tinker or tamper with that work of primitive inspiration, with the image which truth made of itself in the mind of a prophetic era. I should as soon think of touching up the *Cenacle* of da Vinci, or correcting the *Divina Commedia* in the light of critical knowledge of history and science. . . . Our faith is in the revealed truth, not in its translation. . . In all her utterances she (the Church) only repeats the truth revealed—their *meaning* is just the revealed truth which they protect.' Letter to von Hügel, 10 Feb. 1907, *George Tyrrell's Letters*, ed. M. D. Petre, London, 1920, pp. 58–60.

What is obvious is that metaphors used in this primary sense function symbolically: they relate us to a world—whether real or created—and are, therefore, assertions rather than interpretations. But in scripture, as in a Shakespearean tragedy, they are spoken and acted out 'in character'. How, then, are they to be interpreted? In *Lear*, for example, Albany prophesies that, unless 'the heavens' intervene, 'humanity must perforce prey on itself'; Edgar rallies the despairing Gloucester with 'Ripeness is all!' and he tells the dying Edmund, 'The gods are just.' Here the literary critic puts the theologian on his guard: these are not necessarily Shakespeare's judgements. They may be merely 'in character'. Edgar is sententious, and Albany pious. In claiming that this is what *Lear* is about, I cannot go behind the text (to my special knowledge about 'gods'); but I must show whether the text as a whole establishes a particular passage as central, by showing how it is to be read. But how can I know whether life is like this or not? The simple answer—try it!—raises the more important question—what is it that enforces this kind of response? Is it the *language* as such—the peculiar density of metaphor? And does this mean that our response to the primary use of metaphor is performative rather than simply informative or merely aesthetic? In the case of the Bible, the answer seems to be unambiguously yes; and we even claim to be able to infer *true* propositions (or beliefs) from assertions in symbolic and metaphoric form.

What then is the distinction between the literary and the religious use of metaphor? In so far as metaphor and symbol succeed in arousing and convincing our imagination each use succeeds in grasping or showing reality. Each extends our consciousness. In religion, such convictions (or assents) claim also to be compatible with the belief to which they refer, and by which they are authenticated, such as, for example, that Jesus was truly the Son of God. In literature, however, in the strictest sense (as Coleridge noted), a successful metaphor or symbol cannot legitimately claim to do more than to 'suspend' our disbelief in what it realizes. But when a writer does claim to do more than this, is he passing from the literary use of imagination to its religious use? Does the distinction then boil down to one of authority and reality? To *who* says it and to *what* it refers? Kierkegaard thought it did:

When Christ says, 'There is an eternal life'; and when a theological student says, 'There is an eternal life': both say the same thing. . . . both statements are, judged aesthetically, equally good. And yet there is an eternal qualitative difference between them![57]

As I have already pointed out, St. Paul, in describing the Church, disregards mixed metaphors, since they refer to a common referent whose reality and authority are never in question. The same is true of Andrewes, of Shakespeare, and of the Metaphysical poets. Would their metaphors be as dense as they are, if the referent had less authority or reality? And is the second, or projective, use of metaphor the inevitable result, when that authority or reality can no longer be taken for granted?

We have reached the limits of literary criticism, if not moved beyond them. The questions raised need to be stated in a different form. Between ourselves and the Elizabethan and Caroline poets and theologians exists a change in consciousness, describe it how we will—as a dissociation of sensibility, the rise of scientific rationalism, or the birth of the machines. Is the divide unique, or can we remain in continuity? Have we now to say that all metaphors are but projections which require correction, or—if we follow Marx—reduction to the contradiction they reveal in their secular basis? If so, then the first use of metaphor has been superseded, and the distinction I have been drawing, although permissible for purposes of literary history, is chronological merely: the first use of metaphor is chronologically, but no longer logically, prior to the second.

The problem, however, is as much theological as literary. Restated in theological form, it points (I suggest) to a distinction between *holding* a belief and *explaining* it. Does holding a belief depend upon our being able to explain it—has a belief now to be rationally plausible before it can be entertained, or is holding a belief still logically prior to explaining it?

(IV) NEWMAN, MAURICE, AND THE CHRONOLOGY OF BELIEF

i

The theological form of the literary question—does holding a

[57] Soren Kierkegaard, *Of the Difference between a Genius and an Apostle* (1847), E. T. A. Dru, London, 1972, p. 117.

belief now depend upon successfully explaining it?—suggests that if there is a chronology of metaphor, there may also be a comparable chronology of belief. To put it more simply, has there been an *inversion* of priorities in religion? Must we first explain before we may assent? Does reason now have priority over faith? If, as T. S. Eliot has argued, literary and theological adequacy are uniquely related in the seventeenth century and in the Metaphysical poets in particular, is it true that this relationship or grammar common to poets and divines not only disappeared in succeeding centuries, but is incapable of being restored?

What such an argument overlooks is that this common grammar and the priorities it presupposes survives, uninverted, for much longer into the nineteenth century than is commonly supposed. The terms on which it survives take us to the heart of the relationship between religion and imagination; and it is puzzling that Eliot himself does not directly refer to this, since he finds his theological grammar as much in Newman as in Pascal. Newman's questions are his—how can I believe what I cannot understand, or absolutely prove?[58] But Newman does not stand alone. If we seek a theology nourished by a literary culture and an enriched imagination, it has not to be created, but uncovered. It is, furthermore, a theology practised by men as various as Keble, Acton, Simpson, and R. H. Hutton, whose writings show a consistent literary adequacy or 'urbanity' (as Arnold himself noted when referring to Newman's style and to Acton's conduct of the *Home and Foreign Review*[59]).

In Coleridge and Newman it achieves classic expression. Newman himself notes that what drew him from a strict Evangelicalism was his interest in 'the literature of religion'. It was this which led him to the Fathers and to the Caroline divines and Andrewes in particular: even his opponents in the Roman Church characterized his theology—in order to deprecate it— as 'patristic and literary'. But, as I have said, Newman was not alone: contemporary commentators on the ethos of the Movement note its pronounced literary quality,[60] and note also the

[58] As cited in C. S. Dessain, *John Henry Newman*, London, 1966, p. 148.

[59] In the first and second of the *Essays in Criticism* of 1865.

[60] T. Mozley, *Reminiscences*, 1882, ii. 422–3; see also T. M. Parker on the rediscovery of the Fathers in Coulson and Allchin edd., *The Rediscovery of Newman*, London, 1967, pp. 3–5.

disappearance of this characteristically literary ethos in the theology which followed. This was the strong therapy of the old classical education. And even when, on becoming a Catholic, he is choosing a religious order, Newman eschews the Vincentians, for example, as not giving 'to theology and literature that place in their system which we wished'.[61]

In one respect the Oxford Movement does for England what Schleiermacher did for Germany: it provides the theological programme of Romanticism, if we interpret Romanticism as restoring a conception of Nature, not as dead and exploitable, but as a divine sacramental language.[62] But there are two differences, which, taken together, account for its comparative failure either to influence the religious sensibility of its time, or to be recognized for what it was—a restoration of that union of religion and imagination which characterizes the seventeenth-century sensibility. The first difference is that, although the Movement began as a protest against the rationalizing tendencies of German theology, Newman alone gave sufficient emphasis to the need for belief to be adequate to the changed conditions of consciousness and rationality. The second difference was fatal: the effort to answer German rationalism, although at first uniting in a common cause such minds as Newman and Maurice, succumbed before Newman's decision to join the Roman Church—a move which effectively concealed beneath a curtain of polemic the significance of his investigations and method as a theologian. It was Pattison's opinion that, after 1845, in a 'sudden withdrawal of all reverence for the past', Oxford abandoned Coleridge, Kantian logic, and 'sacerdotal principles'.[63]

Worse followed, in that Newman's very method—patristic and literary—was itself suspect at Rome, where the concern to render theology a 'science' (or mirror-image of the prevailing rationalism) as effectively shielded Newman from influence in the Church he joined, as in that he had left. We can now afford to take a more eirenic view. We have also suffered to the full the consequences, nearly fatal to theology, of the subsequent di-

[61] *Newman the Oratorian*, Dublin, 1969, ed. P. Murray, p. 81.
[62] See A. M. Allchin in *The Rediscovery of Newman*, p. 54.
[63] Mark Pattison, *Memoirs*, London, 1885, pp. 240, 166.

vergence in all the European Churches of religion from imagination.

If we begin in 1835, not with Newman in isolation, but with
Newman and Maurice together, we shall retain an understanding of the general and persistent nature of the problem Newman
faced: can we continue to talk of a unique change of consciousness, or even of a dissociation of sensibility, if we are unable to
say more today than what was said yesterday? For example,
readers of contemporary theology and, in particular, of the
dialogue between Karl Barth and Hans Küng on whether
analogy may be properly conceived as '*the* crucial invention of
Anti-Christ',[64] may find in Maurice and Newman sufficient to
make them reconsider this question.

Maurice's first major work, *Subscription no Bondage* (1835), is
immediately concerned with the grounds on which a subscription to the thirty-nine articles of religion may properly be
required. But its more fundamental purpose is to ask what form
a profession of faith should take. Is it of a set of articles or
religious propositions? Maurice's denial leads him to develop
an argument against rationalism which remains important; and
we can see why Newman valued it, as did Maurice himself. He
wrote in the year he died: 'no book which I have written
expresses more strongly what then were, and what still are, my
deepest convictions.'[65]

Because, as Maurice said,[66] it continues his defence 'of
Coleridge's metaphysics and Wordsworth's poetry against the
Utilitarian teaching', the argument of *Subscription no Bondage* not
only has a prophetic ring; it is likely to appeal to a wider
audience than theologians.

Maurice begins by pointing out that the Bible has mistakenly
been held to be 'a set of propository articles'. This is a 'great
fiction'.[67] We must distinguish at once between the language of
scripture and the Creeds (which are professions of personal

[64] Hans Küng, *Justification*, London, 1964, p. 3, citing Barth's original preface to
Church Dogmatics.

[65] *Life of Frederick Denison Maurice*, 1884, i. 174. See also an entry in Dean Church's
notebook (*c*.1836/7) which reads: 'there is something in Maurice, and his master
Coleridge, which wakens thought in me more than any other writings almost' (*Life and
Letters of Dean Church*, ed. Mary C. Church, 1895, p. 17).

[66] *Life*, i. 176.

[67] *Sub.*, p. 84.

faith in God) and Articles of religion (which are merely 'a set of formal propositions'). The growth of such rationalism is the direct effect of the controversy of the sixteenth century. 'Wherever Protestantism prevailed', he says, 'logical propositions prevailed likewise . . . to the banishment of all ancient forms and symbols.' Each week the Reformers were obliged to answer some papal manifesto; and each succeeding controversy deepened the 'shades of doctrine which distinguished them from each other'.[68]

A further consequence was the diminution of the language of prayer and worship into abstractions. The preachers of the seventeenth century had a less subtle logic than their predecessors, 'because in that age devotional forms were disregarded, Creeds and Liturgies were esteemed a bondage, and therefore Articles became all in all the meat, drink, and clothing of the soul'.[69]

The consequent emphasis upon plain and abstract conceptions, far from making for greater understanding had the reverse effect—the abstract phraseology of articles being as unintelligible to simple people as a learned phraseology.[70] A further consequence was that the language of theology became less dependent upon that of prayer and worship, and more upon that of traders and lawyers—a point which Matthew Arnold was to make some thirty-five years later in *St. Paul and Protestantism*. We must return, says Maurice, to those 'hardy conditions of thought' and reverence for ancient forms drawn up in times 'when commerce and jurisprudence themselves derived their life and sustenance from theology'.[71]

In other words, religious subscription is to what is 'dilated in scripture, (and) contracted in the Creed'. I quote Bramhall as he is cited by Newman in *Tract XC*[72] to show to what extent Newman and Maurice share a common presupposition. In fact, Maurice goes so far as to quote Newman in support of his criticism of the rationalist reduction of language, citing the example of the Arians who, by ignoring the symbolic sense of

---

[68] *Sub.*, pp. 5, 6.
[69] *Sub.*, p. 90. Coleridge's point, see above, p. 16.
[70] *Sub.*, p. 91.
[71] *Sub.*, p. 96. For Arnold, see below, p. 98.
[72] *VM* ii. 278.

the words *Father* and *Son*, emphasized exclusively their literal and material sense.[73]

This is a powerful argument never more necessary than in the ecumenical climate of today. It implies that by insisting upon 'plain and literal' statements of what we hold, we may be imposing conditions of conceptual distinctness greater than in the past Christianity has required or believed it ought to require. Furthermore, the harder and stricter, conceptually, the preconditions for belief, the greater our sense of their rational inadequacy, when we discover how much of what we believe cannot be so expressed. The effect of dogmatic theology was, historically, to produce the rational theology of later centuries, which, in turn, was succeeded by pure rationalism and simple scepticism.

Even so, Maurice's argument is not necessarily one against religious subscription, as such (although he seemed to have thought so, and to have adopted what, nowadays, might be termed an extreme Barthian position). His argument holds still against equating such statements as the thirty-nine articles with the traditional symbolical formulations of faith, or equating uniformity of belief with unity of faith.

ii

For Maurice, the words which adequately profess our faith are the symbolically charged language of scripture and creeds, since these are addressed 'to that heart and conscience, which are the common inheritance of all'.[74] To respond to scripture as we should is to discover that 'the text seems brighter and clearer than the comment'. And if we think that the Creed is merely an older form of later articles of religion, we overlook its placing within the context of worship 'in the midst of confessions, prayers, thanksgivings, which interpret its use'.[75] What I believe in 'is not a certain scheme of divinity, but a name—a

---

[73] 'Arius commenced his heresy by taking the *literal* and material sense of the words *Father* and *Son* as the basis of a logical argument, and he was led on to deny their *primary* and *essential* signification, and ultimately to reduce them to a mere metaphor. And yet it is said that Theology has nothing to do with Philology: correctness in science is quite independent of Orthodoxy in doctrine. See Newman's *Arians of the Fourth Century*, cap ii, para v' (*Sub.*, p. 53).

[74] *Sub*. pp. 6, 26.

[75] *Sermons on the Prayer Book*, 1893, p. 148.

Father, who has made the heaven and the earth. . . . The creed is (therefore) an act of allegiance or affiance.'[76]

Thus, to have correct beliefs must be distinguished from knowing or holding the truth. What we hold, we hold—in the primary sense—not as propositions, but *doxologically*, that is in the prayer of praise, memory, and hope—from which doctrinal or metaphysical forms are but inferences.[77] This corresponds to the primary use of metaphor in literature, the implication being that this, the primary language of religious affirmation, must be comparably rich and dense. Thus, the Creed, our prayers, the liturgy are an order of signs—signs of the universal society, and 'the very voice in which God speaks to his creatures'. We must hold them initially in a personal unity; and that order of signs taken in its unity is the Church, which is called Catholic because it is intended to be universal in the fellowship it effects.[78] Because Revelation is 'the actual unveiling of a Person to the conscience, heart, reason of human beings', its character is that of personal relationship. It cannot be reduced to propositions. Its truth must be kept 'from all verbal invasions' and from what he calls 'the vulgar incantation "this only means"'.[79] To speak otherwise is as much a nonsense as 'to speak of loving this lady and her children in the agreement with or the assent to certain propositions'.[80]

The difference between Maurice and Newman now emerges. It was there from the start in their early days as fellow Anglicans. For Maurice the assent of faith, although prehensively wide, is simple; for Newman it is 'one complex act both of inference and of assent'.[81] But so is the act of falling in love, unless we restrict ourselves to love at first sight. In the words of D. H. Lawrence, love has to be learned, and as Jane Austen shows (particularly in *Emma*), we can fail to recognize

---

[76] *The Kingdom of Christ*, ed. A. R. Vidler, 1958, ii. 20.

[77] Cp. E. Schlink, *The Coming Christ and the Coming Church*, Edinburgh, 1967, p. 42: 'The statements of doxology are ultimate, and man cannot go beyond them.' Schlink argues, with Maurice, that doctrinal formulations derive from 'propositions employed in doxology'. For another contemporary discussion, see Nicholas Lash, *Credal affirmation as a criterion Church Membership* in the Tenth Downside Symposium, *Inter-communion and Church Membership*, ed. Kent and Murray, London, 1973, esp. p. 61.

[78] *Kingdom of Christ*, ii. 98, 363.

[79] *Sub*. p. 31; see *What is Revelation?* pp. 107, 211.

[80] *The Epistles of St. John* (1857), London, 1881, pp. 320–1.

[81] *GA*, p. 374.

love when it is concealed by an habitual friendship that is taken for granted. 'Knowledge', as Newman says, 'must ever precede the exercise of the affections.'[82]

Newman's conception of religious certitude is as strong as Maurice's and of a similar character. But such certitude is, for him, the reward, not the pre-condition of faith, and although the image of Christ 'both creates faith and then rewards it', he held that an assent to religious objects, as if they were objects of sight was not directly available for the asking, so to speak, but was the privilege of a devout nation only, 'and such a faith does not suit the genius of modern England'.[83]

The vividness and depth with which we realize the objects of faith depends therefore upon the ideas and conceptions we have and bring to them. Although 'it may be readily granted that the intellectual representation should ever be subordinate to the cultivation of the religious affections', such 'intellectual expression of theological truth not only excludes heresy, but directly assists the acts of religious worship and obedience'.[84] Unless, therefore, the 'ideas which the experience of life affords . . ., however inadequate, be correctly applied to it (the object of faith), they re-act upon the affections and deprave the religious principle'.[85] In the *Parochial Sermons*, Newman is even sharper. 'Forms,' he says, 'are the very food of faith . . .' and being 'precise and definite . . . once broken, they are altogether broken.'[86]

To insist that some form of religious subscription or explanation is no part of the profession of faith is to deny, in the larger sense, that our experience of God is knowledge, and that faith is an intellectual act. This is to allow the mythological and doxological forms of faith to depend unreservedly upon a particular culture, so that should we lose our culture (as may now be thought to be the case) we lose our religion.

iii

Both Newman and Maurice agree that, when we profess our faith, we are holding what is dilated within scripture and con-

[82] *GA*, p. 91.
[83] *GA*, p. 43.
[84] *Arians*, pp. 145–6.
[85] *Arians*, pp. 144–5.
[86] *PPS* iii (1836), 195, 201.

tracted within the Creeds. And in each case, directly we begin, for whatever reason, to explain what we are doing or what it implies or why we should be doing it, then we are involved in ambiguities.

We can accept these ambiguities, ecclesiastically, as forms of accommodation, which allow (as historically they have allowed) the widest comprehension of people and opinions; or, intellectually, as forms of accommodation, which acknowledge that what we are professing cannot be confined to the exactitude of literal and propositional statement.

Nevertheless, unless limits are set to such ambiguities, ecclesiastical or intellectual, we shall never know whether we are bathing a baby or baptizing it, or what we are effecting when we offer the Eucharist. Scholasticism, rationalism, and over-systematization are one set of evils, but mindless euphoria, fanaticism, and neurosis are another, and one which is more likely to afflict us today. Hence, we must endeavour to make some distinction between *holding* and *explaining* our profession of faith.

In the early days of the Oxford Movement this distinction was more taken for granted than it was to be later. Thus, William Froude, in speaking of his brother, Richard Hurrell Froude, says that he then shared with him the ability to take a doctrine on trust, 'without trying to see what I meant by the words I used'.[87] Maurice, on the other hand, did not modify his position; and he felt obliged to oppose Newman's subsequent distinction in the *Grammar of Assent*, when it was published in 1870. Newman draws a firm distinction between dogma, which is 'discerned, rested in, and appropriated as a reality, by the religious imagination', and the same dogma 'held as a truth, by the theological intellect'.[88] This distinction would oblige us to hold such a proposition as, for example, that there is One Personal and present God in two distinct ways: 'either as a theological truth, or as a religious fact or reality. The notion and the reality assented to are represented by one and the same proposition, but serve as distinct interpretations of it.'[89] Although we seem obliged to distinguish a first-order use of

[87] Letter from William Froude to Newman, 16 Apr. 1864 (*Letters*, xxi. 96).
[88] *GA*, p. 75.
[89] *GA*, p. 91.

religious language—that of faith, imagination, and worship—
from a second-order use—that of belief, profession, and explanation—it is as important to preserve the connection as to
make the distinction.

As early as 1833 Newman conceded that 'a system of doctrine
provides 'not a consistent, but a connected statement', but
reliable explanations are essential, if we are to be preserved
from errors of thought, act, and worship.[90]

I would also wish to argue that this distinction, implying a
connection, between *holding* and *explaining* a belief is not subsequent to scripture and the Creeds, but is to be found within
them. The language of scripture frequently (but not always)
takes the form desired by Maurice—that of what I have called
the primary use of metaphor and symbol when, by means of the
parables or of such stories as that of Abraham and Isaac, we are
found by a divine disclosure and are required to believe *in* a
Person.

But the language of the Creeds, especially a conciliar creed
like the Nicene, is already acting in a different way metaphorically. Although we are commanded to believe *in* God, we
are also to believe *that* Christ was of one substance with the
Father. Already we can begin to feel the pressure towards
interpretation and conceptualization. This is notwithstanding
that our response to such language must remain primarily
doxological.

But to stand, as we do, within a pluralist and secular society is
not only to move from light into darkness, but to discover that
the questions are changed and that the priorities seem to be
reversed. From this standpoint, or context, the demand is that
what we believe must be, in the first place, not doxologically or
dogmatically credible, but rationally adequate; and the onus
of proof, in this sense, has rested on the believer since about
1860.[91] This is exactly parallel to the literary dilemma
discussed in the last chapter—if the primary use of metaphor
(in its Shakespearean and metaphysical density) is superseded,
then it is merely chronologically, and no longer logically, prior
to the second or reflective use of metaphor. Similarly, the

---

[90] *Arians*, p. 146.
[91] Newman in a manuscript note (A.30.11) dated 12 Jan 1860, when he was trying to
define the questions which became the starting-point for his *Grammar of Assent*.

primary forms of religious affirmation (in their doxological and dogmatic density) are chronologically, but no longer logically, prior to religious explanations in propositional form. If the chronology of metaphor parallels the chronology of belief, then when the modernist theologian, George Tyrrell, was obliged by the *zeitgeist* to ask, 'what is the truth-function of analogues?' he seemed to have no alternative but to turn from the question in despair, since if, between the language of faith and the language of belief, there is no analogical connection, there can only be an unbridgeable distinction. And it is this despair which separates the modernists from Newman, as it has separated Karl Barth from his critics.

We are now, therefore, more conscious of the need for reliable inferences than for striking metaphors. To speak of placing ourselves within an order of signs to which we respond doxologically will not do, if this seems to evade the question 'how are religious propositions true?' In a society in which the signs, ceremonies, and forms of a religion become increasingly socially implausible, we need some advance guarantees (or reliable inferences) that what we propose to hold is not an indulgence in fantasy, neurosis, or mindless irrationalism.

The problem we now face is that of re-locating our religious explanations within a culture (or grammar) which is no longer confessionally Christian or even religious, but is secular and diverse. And although the sound words we seek, instead of depraving the religious principle must help it to live *semper et ubique et ab omnibus*, such words lose substance and reality to the extent that they fail to explain and, by explaining, to extend the range and depth of the beliefs by which our secular society lives. In this sense the meaning of religious beliefs is contextually determined: how they are used culturally determines their *sense* theologically.[92]

Neverthless, we must, as Maurice insists, hold to the right order of priority. We must never deny language its full capacity to be 'streaked with the light of truths just rising above the horizon'.[93] Not for nothing was he the disciple of Coleridge and a professor of English before he became a professor of Theology.

[92] See Wittgenstein's warning that it is how a term is used in other languages-games that determines its sense in its own language-game (*Remarks on the Foundation of Mathematics*, 1956, pt. IV, sect. 2, p. 133).

[93] *Sub.*, p. 40.

To read him is to discover why we must re-locate a proper and urgent demand for 'plain, literal, and grammatical' inferences within their wider context of the symbolic and metaphorical use of language in scripture and creed. It is a context which, precisely because it is in the Maurician sense a prehensive unity, establishes a limit to rational inference, while (in the literary critical sense) extending the grammar. Yet, from the dark side of a rigorous secularity, what we hold may appear to be only what we agree not to explain away. And it is interesting to ask why, in the seventeenth century, a position of this kind was more readily acceptable than in the nineteenth century. This is how Archbishop Ussher, for instance, interprets subscription to the Articles. They are not to be rejected by any man 'at his pleasure'; 'yet neither do we look upon them as essentials of saving faith, or legacies of Christ and the Apostles; but (as) a mean, as pious opinions fitted for the preservation of unity; neither do we oblige any man to believe them, *but only not to contradict them.*'[94]

It is necessary to remember that in the sixteenth and seventeenth centuries the terms 'plain', 'literal', and 'grammatical' were not understood as excluding or superseding the metaphorical and symbolic uses of language, such as are to be found in scripture and creed. In fact, the contrary was the case: sometimes, the figurative meaning *is* the literal meaning, and cannot be separated from it;[95] and it was only as Rationalism grew that the *univocal* interpretation, unchecked by other uses of language, became dominant. But the obstinate objection has persisted—our language achieves its greatest range and precision, not in the plain and literal style of Francis Bacon, but in the densely metaphorical style of Shakespeare and Donne.

In some respects we are back, today, where the Reformers started, in a situation where (in the words of T. S. Eliot), words slip, slide, perish, will not stand still, when we get the better of words only for what we no longer want to say, and find ourselves on the edge of a grimpen, risking enchantment. In such circumstances, as the members of the liturgical community ap-

[94] See H. H. Henson, *The Church of England*, Cambridge, 1939, p. 98 (my italics).

[95] John Donne asserts that 'the literall sense is alwayes to be preserved', since it is 'the principall intention of the Holy Ghost. . . . And his principall intention in many places, is to expresse things by allegories; by figures; so that in many places of Scripture, a figurative sense is the literall sense' (*Sermons*, ed. Potter and Simpson, 1953, vi. 62).

proach 'the table of God's word', a successful attempt to explain plainly and literally what they have been doing and gaining is not merely enabling them to believe more fully, it may be essential to maintaining their faith. In the darkest sense, reliable inferences and adequate religious propositions succeed only as they locate the metaphors and symbols of religion within a public language growing increasingly negative, even hostile. And subscription to such inferences and propositions is not bondage but liberation. Belief seeks understanding; and weak belief seeks rational sanctions. Yet, although in the lightest and ultimately prior sense, we hold with Maurice (and St. Paul) that Christ came to establish a kingdom, not to proclaim a set of opinions, the difficulty is only partially resolved. If *holding* a belief does not depend upon first successfully *explaining* it, what does it now depend on? *How*, today, do we hold a belief?

Where Newman stands alone is in his concentration upon this as the crucial difficulty for succeeding generations, viz., that circumstances now seem to require us to seek reliable inferences and explanations *before* (and as a condition of) holding the dogmas of faith as convictions by which to live and pray. It was his perception of this apparent inversion of priorities which led Newman to those reflections which are partly published in his essay in aid of a grammar of assent.[96] Newman's achievement is to elucidate the principles by which the proper priority may still be exercised. Undeceived by the chronology of metaphor and of belief, he grounds belief in imagination, but argues also that reliable inferences are not neutral but converge and accumulate. In so doing they authenticate our imaginative assents, and we become certain of what we cannot absolutely prove: 'we know that we know.'[97]

[96] See Newman, *OUS*, pp. 202, 183, 187 on the common, but mistaken, assumption that the act of faith must follow from and be grounded upon an act of reason, and his discussion of this as an example of confusing the *ordo chronologicus* with the *ordo logicus* in *Letters*, xii. 31, 8 Feb. 1847.
[97] *GA*, p. 149.

2

Newman's Grammar of Imagination and Belief

I. Imaginative Assent

(1) BEGINNING WITH ASSENT

The chief contention or grammatical principle of this book is that religious belief originates in that activity we call imagination, and that its verification thus depends now, as in the past, upon its first being made credible to imagination. The phrase (and claim) are Newman's: and in the book which, from the start, he was most concerned to write, he grounds his argument upon this association of imagination and belief. Thus, in writing of belief in the *Grammar of Assent*, he asks: 'Can I rise to what I have called an imaginative apprehension of it?'[1] This power, when awakened, arouses the faculties to act; but 'it leads to practice *indirectly* [my italics] by the action of its object upon the affections'. It is when imagination is allied to belief that men of sufficient energy arise to be 'heroes and saints, great leaders, statesmen, preachers, and reformers' ... but also to be 'visionaries, fanatics, knight-errants, demagogues, and adventurers'. Here is the problem: men are moved to act not by notions but by what seizes their imagination; and Newman grounds his conception of notional and real assent upon this distinction between what might be called an armchair nod of agreement and the decision to go and do something about it.

Newman's originality is in the weight he attaches to what remains the crucial objection—that a belief cannot be held *before* it is proved to be true and certain. How, he asks, are we entitled to hold a belief which we cannot adequately explain? It is in answering this question that Newman finds himself having to appeal to imagination. Why does he think such an appeal necessary; and what does he understand by 'imagination'?

From the standpoint of Newman scholarship what has been said and discussed so far is an essential preparation for answering both these questions, and especially for understanding what

[1] *GA*, pp. 78, 63, 67.

Newman meant by 'imagination'. It is certainly not an appeal to a simple process of 'imaging'; and it is for this reason that I have argued that Newman's originality can be fully appreciated only as we approach him by means of those questions about belief which haunt us still. The priority of imagination must be established within a full and continuing historical perspective if we are to grasp the dimensions or dynamic range which Newman's argument requires for its interpretation; and it is only as we come to him after reading Coleridge, Matthew Arnold, and T. S. Eliot, and as a consequence of such study, that what he has to say about belief and imagination acquires its proper depth and focus. This seems also to have been the view of Gerard Manley Hopkins who, on first reading the *Grammar of Assent* in 1873, wrote: 'What dissatisfies me (in point of style) is a narrow circle of instance and quotation—in a man too of great learning and of general reading.'[2]

On his return from Ireland in 1857, Newman had hoped to get on with a book on metaphysics. In his letters he refers to his wish to deal with what he defines significantly as 'an argument for theism, and a review of the mythical theory of gospel history'.[3] But his efforts with *The Rambler*, and the reception accorded *On Consulting the Faithful in matters of Doctrine*, blocked all chances of his writing on theology and philosophy for publication. Nevertheless, he began a philosophical notebook. From this and other manuscript sources[4] it is possible to see that for a time (around 1860) Newman was pursuing two approaches in parallel, the first being the more obvious conception of the problem as that of the *evidences* for religious belief.

He describes his position at this period as trying to get into a fort, or as finding his way in a labyrinth—a reference not so much to the answers or evidences he sought as to how the question ought to be defined. It was in 1866 amidst the

---

[2] *Further letters of G. M. Hopkins*, ed. C. C. Abbott, 2nd edn., OUP, 1956, p. 58.

[3] *Letters*, xviii, 326.

[4] Referred to as *O*. These papers, covering the years 1846–65, are listed by Newman in a note of 30 Oct. 1870 (*Autobiographical Writings*, ed. Henry Tristram, London, 1956, p. 269f), and are chiefly to be found in the Birmingham Oratory archives in packets B.9.11, B.7.4, A.23.1, and A.30.11. A selection has recently been published as *The Theological Papers of John Henry Newman on Faith and Certainty*, partly prepared for publication by Hugo M. de Achaval, S.J., selected and edited by J. Derek Holmes with a note of introduction by Charles Stephen Dessain, Clarendon Press, 1976, hereinafter referred to as *O (T . . .)*.

significantly romantic surroundings of Glion over Lake Geneva, that Newman suddenly saw the question in a new light.[5] He must begin, not with certitude, or even religious belief, but with common or garden 'assent', where, in order to act you must assume, and that assumption is certain. In very ordinary matters—such as believing that the sun will rise tomorrow, that we live on an island, or that I shall die—I believe myself to be certain. The ambiguity in the use of belief— to imply the deliberate suppression of a doubt—is here set aside. Instead, the question becomes—what has happened, when I say that 'I am certain', or 'I believe'—and mean it? Then the question becomes not *what* verifies, but *how* (since verification has taken place) does it happen? How does the proof work, when the evidence on which we are certain, although sufficient, is logically never guaranteed to be so?

Newman's position is like that of a man who, finding himself outside the door of Doubting Castle, is not quite sure how he has escaped or whether, in fact, he has even been captive. Isaac Newton's difficulty, for example, may be more general than we suppose—when he saw the truth, it was all of a heap, by one act: his great trouble was 'to *find* his proofs'.[6] In such a case, verification has occurred; the problem is *how* it happened. Newman's discovery may be stated thus: 'Let the assent teach you the grammar.'

Part of the difficulty is resolved when we notice that we may be deceived by simple verbal ambiguities For example, 'conclusion' refers both to a state of mind and to inferences drawn from a proposition; and Newman's initial discovery is that 'verification' also has a double sense, since it is applicable to two quite distinct modes, and confusion arises when we require from one mode a form of verification appropriate only to the other. This distinction is most clearly made in a memorandum in dialogue form with William Froude on 14 December 1860.[7]

3. He said that the deepest science-men thought nothing proved, not Newton's theory, etc.

I said that such 'ἐποχὴ (suspension of judgement) was part of the *calculus* as it were of science. It was a rule of the game, or of the court. As all communities, societies, clubs, etc. have rules which are ex-

[5] *Letters*, xxii. 274, and xxv. 199.
[6] W. Ward, *Life of John Henry, Cardinal Newman*, London, 1912, ii. 250; *N*. ii. 73, 5.
[7] *Letters*, xix. 441.

pedient for themselves and for the prosecution of their peculiar objects, so such scepticism was one of the necessary exercises of Reason in those processes which were peculiar to itself.

4. He said that no truth had been arrived at without this habit of sceptical caution—it was the parent of discovery.

I said no great thing would be done without the very reverse habit, viz. that of conviction and faith. Indeed it is obvious that *devotion* cannot exist without it—nor can any sustained course of action *Possunt quia posse videntur.*

5. He said that in his own life, he had suffered from believing too much—never from believing too little.

6. I agreed to his position so far as to allow that much harm came from easiness of belief; but this only showed that faith could have an excess. . . . I might apply what Aristotle says of the mathematician and rhetorician—faith being necessary in matters of practice and conduct, scepticism in matters of speculation.

The explanatory models for this distinction are not confined to the *Grammar of Assent*: they are scattered through Newman's letters, memoranda, and notebooks. What they seem to have in common is the way in which they avoid the simple solution that, in matters of assent, and of religious assent in particular, we make a *leap of faith*. In the *Grammar of Assent*, for instance, Newman uses the relation of the expanding polygon and its enclosing circle to establish the point that verification is not so much a leap as a process in which no ultimate climax can be anticipated; it varies with the individual person and with 'the strength, variety or multiplicity of premises'. Similarly, the peasant who is weather-wise and the physician who excels in diagnoses are not wholly conscious of the steps; they both feel 'all at once and together the force of various combined phenomena'. But this does not weaken their confidence in their predictive capacity.[8]

Certainties, therefore, occur, and it may be, as Berkeley suggests, that it is philosophers alone who suffer from *radical* doubt, first raising a dust and then complaining that they cannot see. For Newman the question takes the form that it does for Levin at the conclusion of *Anna Karenina*: on what grounds is the common man entitled to hold beliefs as certain? The *Grammar of Assent* was conceived, therefore, not as a strictly philosophical treatise on belief, but as a statement of the

[8] *GA*, pp. 243–4; *GA*, p. 252.

grounds on which the uneducated man has as much right to be certain 'as a learned theologian who knows the scientific evidence'.[9] It was therefore addressed 'to such ladies as are bullied by infidels', in order to establish the distinction between faith and prejudice, and to show that the imaginative basis of faith is the same for the simple believer as it is for the converted sceptic.

In the *Grammar of Assent* as we have it Newman is working within certain limits, and it is now possible to supplement his treatment with material from the *Letters* and *Philosophical Notebook*. It is also possible to see how much subtler and more wide-ranging Newman's discussion is than is usually supposed. It is, as it should be philosophically, much more tentative. Yet even his published work on Assent is entitled 'an essay in aid of a grammar'; and I shall argue that Newman's approach is tentative because he understands instinctively how questions must be treated which require an appeal to imagination.

Even so, what is missing in the *Grammar*, as published, is that note of interrogation, so characteristic of his epistolatory style, as in the dialogue with Froude already cited, or in the *Notebook*, where he so frequently argues with himself.[10]

By contrast the style of the *Grammar* is akin to that of the sermons—not so much rhetorical in the pejorative sense, but certainly suasive. A finished argument is being recommended; and this is somewhat to weaken the conviction with which Newman shows his grasp of the essential character of the question he is dealing with—that it is a labyrinth from which we can never wholly escape. Perhaps he recognized this when he admitted that the *Grammar* had not turned out as he had hoped. Since he continued to hold that 'the human mind embraces more than it can master', and is therefore 'unequal to its own

[9] W. Ward, *Life of John Henry, Cardinal Newman*, ii. 243–5, 275.

[10] The late Edward Sillem's introduction to this edition (of the *Philosophical Notebook*) is an essential landmark in Newman studies, because of the way in which it establishes definitively this note of interrogative subtlety as the true characteristic of Newman's method as a philosopher of religion. This is further reinforced by an invaluable analysis of the books and authors Newman had read. It is important to know that he read Leibniz while, at the same time, deprecating the attempts of the later German idealists to reduce explanation to a single principle. The section on the influence of the Romantic movement on Newman is, however, unnecessarily speculative. It was not the obscure Abraham Tucker, but the central figure of Coleridge that directed Newman's attention to the proper questions. And this is a fact that can be established, see my 'How much of Coleridge had Newman read?' in *Newman and the Common Tradition*, Oxford, 1970.

power of apprehension',[11] his epistemology may remain insusceptible of a systematic or even of a philosophically consistent justification. As he said of Coleridge, he aims to provide ' "aids" for our "reflection", not instruments for our compulsion'.[12] We must also not overlook the never-failing suspicion which Newman had to face from fellow Catholic theologians. Even in 1870 he may have felt that only in the solid treatise form of the *Grammar* was he likely to gain a hearing, and even then he rightly anticipated adverse reviews. These were based on the mistaken ground that he held the proofs for the existence of God to be merely probable (in the sense of uncertain), and to rest on the priority of feeling over rational demonstration. His chief critic among the Jesuits, Fr. Thomas Harper, charged Newman with arguing for 'conviction without, or at least above, producible proof'. The suspicion among contemporary Catholics of all arguments grounded upon religious experience, intuition, and 'illuminism' may also have led Newman to devote rather less space than his argument requires to its ground in our awareness of the existence of God. This comes to us, 'in the first instance', from conscience, which reveals 'not only that God is, but what He is'.[13] Instead, as we have seen, he chose to generalize the argument from experience and apply it to what he called 'human' as well as 'religious' certitude.[14]

Although Newman does not avoid his question how what begins as 'an impression on the imagination' becomes 'a system or creed in the reason', he assumes that faith and belief are to each other as implicit to explicit, inarticulate to articulate, and pre-conceptual to conceptual. They modulate into each other, therefore, and may be said to share a common grammar. Thus he does not press the distinction between assents to the primary forms of religious faith (expressed in metaphor, symbol, and story), and to the beliefs and doctrines derived from them. Nor does he distinguish the certitude that there is a reality corresponding to the primary forms from the certitude that the beliefs are true. By beginning with the general condition that all

[11] Anne Mozley, *Letters and Correspondence of John Henry Newman during his Life in the English Church*, London, 1890–1, ii. 311 (1840); cp. *GA*, p. 292.
[12] *GA*, p. 232.
[13] *GA*, p. 296.
[14] *Letters*, xxi. 270.

beliefs—religious, secular, and political—must first be credible to imagination, is he short-circuiting the argument? Or is he, instead, doing proper justice to that 'complex act of inference and of assent' which an appeal to imagination requires? In the latter case he is not alone, but the company he keeps is not that of philosophers or even of theologians (except Maurice), but of poets and literary critics.

He is, for example, anticipated by Coleridge, who writes: 'what we cannot *imagine*, we cannot, in the proper sense of the word, conceive.'[15] Kierkegaard, too, sees imagination as 'what providence uses to get men into reality, into existence, to get them far enough out, or in, or down into existence'. It is what is necessary for man 'to soar higher than the misty precinct of the probable', and is thus 'the faculty *instar omnium*'. Yet, in so being, it does not take the place of reason and other faculties, but is the means of their being brought into 'equilibrium' and 'simultaneity'; 'and the medium in which they are unified is existence'.[16] Coleridge, too, writes of imagination as bringing the whole soul of man into activity; and if we turn to the literary usage of imagination we see at once that such descriptions exactly characterize our response: we so respond fully and completely to a tragedy (or a symphony) *before* we seek to explain what it means or to justify our response. Furthermore, in the case of novels or plays we are brought into active engagement with what Coleridge calls an *adunating* power—that is, one able to bring together in a living unity elements which appear to be discordant or even contradictory of each other.

In making an appeal to imagination in the full sense, Newman was obliged to modify or abandon the precise vocabulary of philosophical usage for that of literary criticism. A major influence was Joseph Butler, but the student of Coleridge will find many expressions with which he is already familiar; and the student of literature and its criticism may find Newman's argument more readily intelligible than the philosopher or theologian.

We have already seen the extent to which, in order to describe the successful act of imagination, we are obliged to dis-

---

[15] *Aids to Reflection*, p. 44.
[16] S. Kierkegaard, *The Journals*, E. T. A Dru, New York, Harper Torchbooks, 1959,

pense with the reductive language of philosophy—of plain, literal, and univocal meanings 'about which there is no puzzle', for that of the 'difficult resolution'—of the 'iteration' of metaphor[17] and of apparent contradictions (or 'oscillations') successfully resolved. We seem to require a new or larger vocabulary which will enable us to explain how we are able to live with what, seemingly, are doubts, uncertainties, even projections. We are obliged to describe our way of proceeding not as by inference and strict demonstation, but as by a gradual convergence (or focusing stereoscopically) which induces belief (rather than proving it).

When we see this, we have reached the position that Newman himself reached, when he saw that for a belief to be credible, it must be so primarily to imagination. It is to stand where we should, if we are to begin—*outside* the walls of Doubting Castle. Newman argues, in answer to Hume, that it was not the religious organization or opinions of the early Christians which were responsible for the vitality of their faith, but the *image* of Christ—the original instrument of their conversion—which gave life to their preaching. This it is that brings together truths which 'appear to diverge from each other'.[18] What we respond to is the whole: 'As God is one, so the impression which He gives us of Himself is one; it is not a thing of parts; it is not a system. . . . It is the vision of an object.'[19] This is Christ—'the very Object whom it (the divinely-enlightened mind) desires to love and worship—the Object correlative of its own affections'.[20] This vision or image was what gave life to the first preaching; it was the image of what first creates faith, and then rewards it.[21]

In so talking, Newman's emphasis falls upon the positive aspect of imagination which, by its intensifying and unifying power, enables us to make a whole-hearted, 'energetic', and real assent—'as if we saw'. In other words, we become convinced. But to be convinced is one thing; to know for certain

---

p. 243; *Sickness unto Death*, New York, Anchor, 1954, pp. 163, 174. *Concluding Unscientific Postscript*, Princeton U.P., 1941, p. 311.

[17] See above, p. 21.
[18] *OUS*, p. 27, *GA*, p. 339.
[19] *OUS*, p. 330.
[20] Ibid., p. 236.
[21] *GA*, pp. 352–4, 339.

that there is a reality to correspond is another.[22] Assent and proof are two distinct aspects;[23] assents change, only certitudes endure. Thus, like Othello, Leontes, or Napoleon,[24] we can be convinced, and whole-heartedly assent to our conviction, but be profoundly mistaken. Here Newman shows his understanding of the negative aspect of imagination. Its assents can show themselves to be mere 'projections',[25] which evaporate as soon as they are investigated.

How do we know that there is a reality to correspond to what may be a mere metaphor? How do we distinguish between the convictions of heroes and saints and those of visionaries, fanatics, knight-errants and demagogues?[26] But to raise such questions is to weaken our assent, since directly we supply reasons for assenting, we suggest reasons for not assenting.[27]

Here Newman is on ground made familiar to readers of Arnold, Hardy, and Eliot—the instability of the imaginative process until it is completed or authenticated. Thus 'in its *complete* exhibition keeness in believing is united with repose and persistence'.[28] How, then, do we authenticate our imaginative assents? It is here that Newman draws upon Butler's argument that probability is the guide of life; and the celebrated model derived from Butler—that probabilities accumulate until, by taking the evidence together, we become certain—occurs in Newman's manuscripts as early as 1848. But Newman distinguishes his use from that of Butler, who fails to distinguish between truth (or faith), and practical certainty (or what is safest to be acted on).[29] For Newman the movement from probability to certitude is qualitative; its limit is credibility in the conclusion and certainty in the mind.

Again, from what has already been said about imagination, Newman's distinction is what one would expect: the conclusion

---

[22] 'The fact of the distinctness of the images which are required for real assent, is no warrant for the existence of the objects which those images represent. . . . We have no right to consider that we have apprehended a truth, merely because of the strength of our mental impression of it' (*GA*, p. 61).

[23] *GA*, p. 143.

[24] *GA*, pp. 167, 253; *O* (*T*, p. 113).

[25] *OUS*, p. 325.

[26] See above, p. 46; *GA*, p. 67.

[27] *GA*, p. 164.

[28] *GA*, p. 164 (my italics).

[29] *Letters*, xix, 480; xix. 460.

must retain that strong sense of reality which characterized the original assent: a mere practical certainty is insufficient. This leads Newman to make a further distinction between investigation and inquiry: inquiry is 'inconsistent with assent', since it implies doubt; investigation, on the other hand, is a necessity. 'In the case of educated minds . . . such a trial of their intellects is a law of their nature, like the growth of childhood into manhood'.[30] 'Investigation' is of what we are imaginatively predisposed to believe, in order to distinguish faith from mere prejudice. When we investigate (as distinct from 'inquire into') our imaginative convictions, our purpose is both to establish their reality, and to know that we know. We do so within a structure or context—in religion that of tradition—which determines the nature of the evidence: personal testimonies, reflections upon the acts of those who have lived authentically (the saints), episodes from the history of Christianity, and of the controversies and decrees of the Christian community in particular. Predisposed as we are to accept this evidence as 'reliable' we notice that when it is taken together it converges or coalesces (as in legal logic) rather than demonstrates its necessity (as in scientific logic). It is this convergence of reliable inferences or 'probabilities' which precipitates certitude—I now know that I know.[31] What began as 'an impression on the Imagination has become a system or creed in the Reason'.[32]

This is a method with which we are already familiar in T. S. Eliot and, before him, in Lancelot Andrewes—Christianity is a meeting of virtues which appear to be opposed, but 'sever them, and farewell all'.[33] Kierkegaard, as well as Newman, describes what has been effected as an equilibrium.[34] This is the master principle of Newman's method as a theologian. The truth of one doctrine is established when we see its location or relation to other doctrines: it is their connection, mutually and as a whole, which constitutes their truth. Conversely, he frequently warns his correspondents against taking statements 'of scripture or of Catholic doctrine . . . out of the body of teaching' and placing them 'in antagonism to other statements, instead of (their)

[30] *GA*, pp. 144–5.
[31] *GA*, p. 149.
[32] *Dev.*, p. 49; *OUS*, p. 329.
[33] See above, p. 22.
[34] See above, p. 52.

being viewed as parts of a whole, each interpreting and modifying the next'.[35]

This is a plausible argument, philosophically. In the strict sense all empirical statements, if taken in isolation from each other, are doubtable—e.g. that Britain is an island, or that I shall die—since the evidence for successful induction is never logically sufficient; but when such propositions are taken in relation to other propositions, the evidence 'accumulates', and we become certain that Britain is an island, and that we shall die.[36]

The best illustration of Newman's argument is in his use of the architectural model of the arch. It is found in the notebook, but is most fully described in a letter of 12 February 1861: 'Now, is not the proof of Religion of *this* kind? I liken it to the mechanism of some triumph of skill, tower or spire, geometrical staircase or vaulted roof, where *"Ars est celare artem"*: where all display of strength is carefully avoided, and the weight is ingeniously thrown in a variety of directions, upon supports which are distinct from, or independent of each other.'[37]

D. H. Lawrence in his letters and in his treatment of the Cathedral in *The Rainbow* emphasizes the same point—that when we speak of a sign or symbol, we are properly referring to a structure of interrelated symbolism; and that what we are prepared to be bound by is this interrelated structure as a whole, to which the particular symbolic instance leads us. Thus, 'what think ye of Christ?' invites us to do more than simply decide upon the historicity of Jesus; and if we knew what Shakespeare's conscious intention was when he began to write *Hamlet*, we should still have little more than a way into the expanded metaphors and characters which are the play. To respond to metaphor and symbol is to be bound, not to an instance, but to an interrelationship as a whole; and the ap-

---

[35] *Letters*, xxviii. 133.

[36] See Professor J. M. Cameron's discussion in *Newman-Studien* (*Neunte Folge, Nurnberg, 1974*), his citation of Wittgenstein's *On Certainty*, and Newman's own discussion of how we come to believe in the immortality of the soul, as this is exemplified in the dying factory-girl's affirmation in Mrs Gaskell's *North and South* (*GA*, p. 237).

[37] *Letters*, xix. 480, 460.

propriate form of verification must itself be similarly complex.[38]

(II) DRAWING MANY THINGS INTO ONE

Newman's sharp distinction between assent and inference is anticipated in his earliest writings. 'Reasoning' is restricted to simple inference; and in the *Oxford University Sermons* he distinguishes faith—the creative power, from reason—the critical; the creative being prior to the critical, as implicit is to explicit. We mistake if we assume that the assent of faith is impermissible until we have first successfully demonstrated it to be rationally adequate; instead, what we should be doing is to investigate our convictions, in order to make explicit rationally what is already implicitly certain: 'all men have a reason, but not all men can give a reason'; and clearness in argument 'is not indispensable to reasoning well'.[39] It is the restrictive nature of the argument—that it applies solely to religious faith—which Newman is concerned to correct in the *Grammar of Assent*. Thus he begins, not with the certainty of 'faith', but with ordinary assent—secular, political, religious, or imaginative; and his later argument is grounded upon the distinction between modes of assent, each of which is a cognitive or *rational* act. It is interesting to note that he treats Aquinas's distinction between *intellectus* and *ratio* as being akin to this subsequent distinction between real and notional assent;[40] and the argument is fatally weakened if this distinction is conceived as one between strong and weak assent. Each mode, by presupposing an absolute or certain referent, is making a truth-claim. Thus, in speaking of what is probable, Newman does not mean what is *uncertain*, but what cannot be demonstrated as mathematically or logically

[38] In his last work, *Apocalypse*, Lawrence significantly identifies such a way of thinking with the religious tendencies modern man has suppressed in himself: 'We have to drop our own manner of on-and-on-and-on, from a start to a finish, and allow the mind to move in cycles, or to flit here and there over a cluster of images' (*Apocalypse* (1931), Penguin edn., pp. 50, 54). This way of thinking in metaphors and symbols 'avoids the I and puts aside the egotist. . . . That was how man built the cathedrals. He didn't say, "Out of my breast springs this cathedral!" But "In this vast whole I am a small part, I move and live and have my being".'

'You should try to grasp . . . *the complete whole* which the Celtic symbolism made in its great time. We are such egoistic fools. We see only the *symbol* as a *subjective expression*: as an expression of ourselves. That makes us so sickly when we deal with the old symbols: like Yeats' (*Letters of D. H. Lawrence*, 19 Dec. 1914).

[39] *OUS*, pp. 182–4; p. 259.

[40] *O* (17 June 1846). Newman again discusses the distinction in 1859 (*T*, p. 52).

necessary. The distinction, therefore, is not between a strong or weak form of verification, but between 'different subject matters'[41] and their appropriate modes of proof: 'A man who said "I cannot trust a cable, I must have an iron bar," would, *in certain given cases*, be irrational and unreasonable:—so too is a man who says I must have a rigid demonstration, not moral demonstration, of religious truth.'[42] Thus, to look for the wrong form of verification could be to convict oneself mistakenly of lack of faith, and to deny, for the sake of a theory, our capacity to grow to belief. Probability admits of 'more or less'; and the certitude it precipitates is grown into and not merely or immediately demonstrated—'the measure of probability necessary for certainty varying with the individual mind'.[43]

To speak of being 'grown into' seems to imply a disposition to particular acts or feelings, which are themselves the means of growth. Thus, because 'certitude' differs from 'knowledge, which is the simple contemplation of truth as objective . . . we speak of having knowledge and feeling certain'.[44] This is a very close to H. H. Price's distinction between believing *that* statements are true and believing *in* persons; and in a further note[45] Newman writes: 'To *see* and to *feel* are to *know* and to *believe*.'

When Newman speaks of 'the limit of increasing probabilities' as being 'credibility in the conclusion', he is claiming that the movement from probability to certitude occurs when what is probable becomes credible. But to what? To the reason? This has already been denied. What is credible is what becomes *real* to imagination. But in what sense? to the whole man, or to the man made whole, whose faculties have thus been united in existence? In the *Apologia* Newman speaks of the whole man moving, and of logic as but the paper record of it. Bernard Lonergan notes that 'proof' is an inadequate term for express-

[41] *O*. See appendix to this chapter, where Newman makes this point specifically, pp. 82f. below.

[42] *Letters*, xxi. 146, 6 July 1864.

[43] *Letters*, xi. 288–9; and *N*. i. 178. This is akin to H. H. Price's conclusion that, in matters of religious belief, 'the postulate of unrestricted public verifiability might be false. It might be that in some spheres (though not in the sphere of ordinary sense perception) the cognitive powers which a person has do depend in some way on the kind of person that he is' (*Belief*, London, 1969, p. 472).

[44] *O* (*T*, p. 127), 25 Sept. 1865.

[45] *O* (*T*, p. 20), 16 Dec. 1853, 'on the certainty of faith'.

ing this movement to certitude, whereby, to paraphrase Newman, we make the objects of assent subjectively our own. Lonergan prefers to use the term 'conversion' and, in doing so, quotes with relish a passage written by Newman in 1841 and used in the *Grammar of Assent*: 'Logic makes but a sorry rhetoric with the multitude; first shoot round corners, and you may not despair of converting by a syllogism.'[46]

It is in this sense that we should understand Newman's remarks that Hume's dismissal of the Pentateuch is on the ground that the account is inconceivable to the imagination; and he suggests that it was this challenge that may well have provoked Butler to write the *Analogy*, since the aim of Butler's method and the nature of his success are to 'quiet the imagination' rather than to appeal to the reason.[47]

It is therefore significant that Newman's ultimate model for verification is an incarnational one of the person or 'whole man'. Real assent is neither an act of will which sets aside reasonable doubts, nor a simple reflex action; and although, as it is articulated and analysed, its complexity becomes manifest, it is experienced as free and undetermined. And although the certitude it achieves is grown (rather than reasoned) into, this certitude 'does not admit of more or less—but is a state of mind, definite and complete, admitting only of being and not being. . . . Certitude then does not come under the reasoning faculty; but under the imagination.'[48] Growth to certitude occurs as we 'realize' or articulate our first principles: 'they are the means of proof, and are not proved; they rule and are not ruled. . . . You do not so much appeal to them as act from them.'[49] Why Newman describes the act of real assent as 'imaginative' is because it is by such creative acts that we achieve our personal identity: 'Man begins with nothing realized (to use the word), and he has to make capital for himself by the exercise of those faculties which are his natural inheritance. Thus he gradually advances to the fulness of his original destiny.'[50] As we form our personality, so we bring into being the unique means by which (or the 'world' within which)

[46] *GA.*, p. 71, quoted in Bernard Lonergan, *Method in Theology*, London, 1972, p. 338.
[47] *N.* ii. 109 and *O* (A.30.11), 'The Conceivable'.
[48] *O* (*T*, pp. 124, 126), 20 July 1865.
[49] *Lectures on the Present Position of Catholics*, pp. 260–1.
[50] *GA*, p. 265; cp. Fernandez, *Messages*, pp. 244–5.

our convictions grow into certitude and are authenticated. It is in this sense that Newman, taking as his model the assent of faith in Jesus Christ, generalizes his argument. By giving to the realized human personality a power to become certain of its imaginative assents, he gives it an absolute value. By drawing many things into one, it becomes 'a whole complete in itself'.[51]

(III) WHY CERTITUDE?

What has hitherto passed un-noticed is that in the early drafts of the substance of the *Grammar of Assent* Newman's original distinction was between notional and *imaginative* assent. It is recorded as early as 1863, and is maintained until at least two years before the publication of the *Grammar*, when he writes: 'According as the apprehension is notional or imaginative, so may the assent be called one or the other, the notional assent being languid, and the imaginative energetic.'[52]

Why does Newman later substitute *real* for imaginative? It may be that the substitution clarified the order of our response to faith: we must experience its object as real before we can ask if the belief is true. This is borne out by Newman's remark, after completing the *Essay on the Development of Christian Doctrine*, that 'I believe that *I* was the *first* writer who made *life the* mark of the true Church.'[53]Since this experience of its reality, or life, is prior to and a condition of its verification, the questions about the Christian faith which are uppermost are about its reality— how and on what terms does it continue to live? Do I *know*, or *see*, or *believe* that it is credible? Which? To *know* and to *see* imply appeals simply to reason and to the senses; and these Newman rejects, in favour of an appeal to imagination. This is to *believe* in the sense that I do not see or know in fact: it is *as if* I saw or knew: it is *probably* the case. But is this not to make an illicit transition from 'believing that' to 'believing in', where the second form seems to conceal or concede a prior doubt, which is absent when the first form is used?

As we have seen, Newman's use of 'probable' does not mean 'uncertain', but 'reliable'. Nevertheless, the word can be used to imply either the existence of a doubt or its suppression. It is possible to understand Newman's argument as implying that a

[51] *Historical Sketches*, iii. 41–2.
[52] *O(T*.p. 135). See also p. 83 below (Appendix).
[53] *Letters*, xi. 101.

successful appeal to imagination acts by 'dissipating' a prior doubt, and that it is this imaginative 'diffusion' and 'dissipation' which facilitates belief—hence, perhaps, his distinction in the *Apologia*[54] between ten thousand difficulties and a doubt, in the radical sense of an irresolvable, sceptical uncertainty.

Nevertheless, it is also part of Newman's argument that real assents do not necessarily endure. Convictions are volatile and unstable. If the movement to authentication (or certitude) fails, then we find that we can neither live with the metaphors and symbols which express convictions nor live without them. A movement of oscillation (to be described in Part Two) has begun. Newman argues, as will Eliot, that we cannot remain indefinitely in such a state of oscillation, since it is to be parasitic upon our culture and its inherited beliefs. If we do so, our 'difficulties' become 'doubts'. What we need to know is whether what convinces us is both real and true. Thus imagination, like faith, seeks understanding, in order to give substance and authenticity to its forms: 'forms are the food of faith'.[55] A faith which cannot grow into the certitude of belief may evaporate. It is at risk.

It may be objected that, today, our sense of probability is inevitably weaker than was Newman's: this is the effect of our cultural condition and of what has been described as a change of consciousness; but the intensity with which we suffer uncertainty and doubt does not affect the logic of the argument. What can happen is that we mistakenly over-react to the initial volatility of imaginative assent, and then theorize ourselves into denying our capacity to grow into certitude—political, as well as religious. Although such despair afflicts theologians as well as poets later in the century—Tyrrell, for example, believed that no truth function (or reliable inferences) could be drawn from the metaphors and analogues which expressed the rudiments of faith—directly we turn to literature we realize at once that to speak, in Newman's sense, of the accumulation of probabilities is to speak of something more than a dispassionate weighing up of evidence. It is to suffer anxiety, and ambiguity as we come into the truth—in *Hamlet*, that 'readiness is all', or in *The Brothers Karamazov*, that 'each is responsible for all', and that

---

[54] *Apo.*, p. 332.
[55] See above, p. 40.

only when a grain of wheat falls into the ground and dies, does it bring forth much fruit.

Even so, a difficulty remains. Why does Newman require certitude in the absolute sense? Why does he not settle, as does Joseph Butler, or even George Eliot, for a 'practical' certainty? The answer is suggested in the chapter[56] on Newman and Maurice, where Newman is quoted as saying that forms are the food of faith, and that intellectual expressions of religious truth are necessary, not only against heresy, but to assist acts of religious worship and obedience.

It is sometimes suggested that Newman's need for certitude, or absolute certainty, was psycho-pathological, and that by a reinterpretation of the autobiography we may find the clue. This is at odds with what has already been shown. Newman's need for certitude is religious (in the pastoral and spiritual sense) since, as he says, you cannot worship a probable God[57]— a point made also in the *Grammar of Assent*, when he remarks, 'religion cannot maintain its ground at all without theology. Sentiment, whether imaginative or emotional, falls back upon the intellect for its stay.'[58] In order to be religious, we need to know that we know. We will see in Part Three what happens when faith fails to issue into belief, or when the act of religious imagination remains incomplete, oscillating between two worlds—one dead, the other powerless to be born. Imagination, like faith, seeks understanding, and for the same reasons. But, in religion, once we have attained the certitude necessary for the practice of the religious life of prayer and obedience, some part of our investigation is concluded. We now *know* that we are entitled to profess what, before, we held in spite of its seeming uncertainty and implausibility, when all we could do was to pray, 'I believe, help thou mine unbelief.' Characteristically, Newman illustrates this fact by a matter-of-fact image: 'You cease walking when you have got home—if you went on walking you would get all wrong. *Inquiry* [*sic*] ends, when you at length *know* what you were inquiring about. When the water boils you take the kettle off the fire; else, it would boil away.'[59]

[56] See above, p. 40. See also *T*, p. 35, n.1 on Butler.
[57] *Letters*, xxvii. 188.
[58] *GA*, pp. 92, 149.
[59] *Letters*, xxvii. 161–2. Here Newman seems to forget his distinction between 'investigate' and 'inquire'.

II. From Imagination to Belief

(IV) 'SAYING AND UNSAYING TO A POSITIVE RESULT'

To press the question 'how does what begins as "an impression on the imagination" become a system or creed in the reason?'[60] raises an immediate difficulty. Statements of belief, like all expressions which powerfully affect our imagination, are more often than not highly ambiguous in form. 'It is a a property of depth to lead a writer into verbal contradictions; and it is a property of simplicity not to care to avoid them', Newman writes of statements in scripture;[61] and he frequently requires a distinction to be made between what is simply self-contradictory and what is conceptually 'inconceivable'. He admits that 'the notion of supernatural truths involves contradictions'; and he defines a mystery as 'a statement uniting incompatible notions';[62] but the verbal contradiction to which he is referring is not the same logically as self-contradiction.[63] He does not go so far as Kierkegaard, therefore, who, in speaking of the inevitably paradoxical nature of religious discourse, claims that 'the paradox is not a concession but a category, an ontological definition which expresses the relation between an existing cognitive spirit and eternal truth'.[64]

Ambiguity, polarity, even paradox are inseparable from our attempts at metaphysical or theological statement, since such statements are not primary but derived, being themselves explanatory paraphrases of what is originally expressed in metaphorical or symbolic form. No matter how hard the metaphysician tries to convert 'the light that never was on sea or land' into forms which are less immediately illogical, the words 'slip, slide, perish . . . , will not stay still'. Faced by such polarities as that between 'the perfection of sanctity' and 'the admission of moral evil', or between God's 'sovereignty of will' and his 'toleration of the rebellious', the theologian must resist the temptation to surrender his experience of the transcendent reality to forms which can only partially express it. All we can

---

[60] *Dev.*, pp. 49–50.
[61] *DA*, p. 174.
[62] *GA*, p. 36.
[63] *N.* ii. 105–7; *O* (A.30.11), 'The Conceivable'.
[64] *Journals*, pp. 117–18.

do, as Newman remarks, is to 'put ourselves on the guard as to our proceeding, and protest against it, while we do it. We can only set right one error of expression by another. By this method of antagonism we steady our minds . . . by *saying and unsaying to a positive result*. We lay down that the Supreme Being is omnipresent *or* everywhere, and yet nowhere. . . . He is ineffably one, yet He is exuberantly manifold.'[65]

Once more we are in that field shared with literature. The method by which religious conceptions are fashioned into shape 'by opposite strokes'[66] is not only at the heart of Newman's conception of how doctrines are formed and developed, but of how the separate disciplines which comprise a university establish their respective relations and ranges. It is also the method of prose fiction. And it is especially so where the author wishes to convey religious insights authentically, as in Dostoevsky's *The Brothers Karamazov*. Why has this got to be a long book, in which the characters speak at length, collide with each other, and contradict themselves? Because this, too, has to be a 'saying and unsaying' in order to fashion the meaning adequately, since it is how we come into acquaintance with the fact, which determines whether that fact is realized for us as such, or remains merely a salvific maxim, or significant proposition torn with a rough pastoral hand out of its context in the living fiction.

Because religious utterance has to say so much before it is complete (carrying as it does 'all its separate meanings at

---

[65] *O* (*T*. pp. 101–2), my italics. As early as 1842, in his footnotes to his translation of St. Athanasius, we can see Newman's conception of religious language beginning to form, as when he writes: 'It is sometimes erroneously supposed that such illustrations as this' (Word, Son, Wisdom, Image, etc.) 'are intended to *explain* how the Sacred Mystery in question is possible, whereas they are merely intended to show that the words we use concerning it are not *self-contradictory*, which is the objection most commonly brought against them. To say that the doctrine of the Son's generation does not intrench upon the Father's perfection and immutability, or negative the Son's eternity, seems at first sight inconsistent with what the words Father and Son mean, till another image is adduced, such as the sun and radiance, in which that alleged inconsistency is seen to exist in fact. Here one image corrects another; and the accumulation of images is not, as is often thought, the restless and fruitless effect of the mind to *enter into the Mystery*, but is a *safeguard* against any one image, nay, any collection of images, being supposed *sufficient*' (*Select Treatises of St. Athanasius*, Oxford, 1842–4, i. 43–4).

[66] *Dev.*, p. 411 (cp. p. 51). This is Lancelot Andrewes's point that 'Christianity is a meeting', see above, p. 22.

once'),[67] it has been called 'speaking until the penny drops'. If this seems inadequate, it is because—standing as we are in a field shared with literature—we are faced not by a language starved into notions and drained of its depth,[68] but by the full rigour of an appeal to imagination. This does not oblige us simply to deal in myths, metaphors, and symbols, but to do so 'polysemously', to quote Dante—that is, 'in more senses than one'.[69] In scripture, as in literature, what is said is said in context and 'in character'. Thus, Dostoevsky's 'religion', for example, is to be found neither in Dmitri, nor in Ivan's story of the Grand Inquisitor, nor even in Alyosha, but in their inter-action as characters in a necessarily long novel. The brothers' behaviour, in its violent and unpredictable oscillations from love to hatred, piety to blasphemy, and gentleness to brutality, polarizes 'paratactically'.[70] Yet these extremes are reconciled and unified in their family resemblance—they are all Karamazovs; and what it is to be a Karamazov is realized in the relation of each to all. Only thus, when we have got the balance of the characters right, can we understand *how* suffering frees us from ourselves and enables us to accept responsibility 'for everyone and everything',[71] and what the concluding maxim— 'each is responsible for all'—*signifies*. It also (and almost inci-dentally) enables us to grasp what Russian Orthodoxy means by 'sobornost'—that togetherness of persons committed to be one in Christ.

Although, for the believer, such stories, metaphors, and sym-bols require to be completed ethically—by acting out what they oblige us to perform—they are language forms of a uniquely resistant kind: assertions for which there can be no wholly adequate or sufficient explanation, where, to quote Donne, 'the figurative sense is the literal sense'.[72] In literature, as in reli-gion, they stand for 'ultimate points of vision'; and, in religion, for those realities to which we give the assent of faith, and from which we infer beliefs. Newman cites the image of Christ re-tained by the first believers which reconciled 'conflicting and

[67] Coleridge, *CN* 3628.
[68] *GA*, p. 203.
[69] See above, p. 23
[70] A characteristic noted by Auerbach, *Mimesis*, p. 523. See below, p. 113.
[71] *The Brothers Karamazov*, E. T., Penguin, 1958, i. 377.
[72] See above, p. 44.

divergent descriptions by embodying them in one common representative'.[73] A similar function is performed by the story of Abraham and Isaac, by the primary credal statements that God is our father, and Jesus Christ his son, or by the references in scripture to Jesus as both pastor and agnus, priest and sacrifice.

Referring as they do to what is both similar and dissimilar, their meaning can never be expressed without ambiguity. No inferences or paraphrases can exhaust their significance; and their very ambiguity or paradoxical form seems to preserve them as permanent possibilities of experience: uninvertible, conceptually irreducible, and rudimental. It is in this sense that I have referred to them as analogues.[74]

They enable us to see, initially, by juxtaposition rather than by logical sequence: their meaning emerges as they are taken together—a resolution which has been variously described as a holding in polar tension, or seeing stereoscopically; and as a saying and unsaying, or correction by opposite strokes. These are the ways we describe, respectively, the movement from doubt to faith, and from faith to belief. This is what we observe when Newman, in speaking of the persons of the Trinity, says of the analogue 'Person' that it 'does not tell us more, but enables us to perfect the system by a *distinction*. . . . The word 'Person', then, is both the refutation of an objection, and the confession of an insoluble question.'[75] Similarly, when Eliot writes[76] 'that, to be restored, our sickness must grow worse', he is using illness as the analogue for the experience of our redemption. And Jude's discovery that what was good for God's birds was bad for God's gardener[77] differs only in degree from Abraham's discovery that God wishes him to kill his son. The essential difference is in how such analogues are interpreted.

Newman, as well as Kierkegaard, is very much alive to the significance of the Abraham and Isaac story as a crucial instance of the form in which God's claim upon us has to be expressed. Both interpret it as a way of showing how our understanding is determined and limited by God's dealing towards us. Kierkegaard refers to it as the teleological sus-

[73] *GA*. p. 339 (cp. *OUS*, pp. 27–9).
[74] See above, p. 29f.
[75] *N*. ii. 59, 60, 96, 134, 105.
[76] See below, p. 119.
[77] See below, p. 106.

pension of the ethical. Newman is characteristically cooler: 'But to say that nothing is possible in God but what we have had experience of, already, is a form of Hume's argument against miracles, and must be refuted as that is refuted.' To expect God to deal with us as we are expected to deal with him is 'another kind of anthropomorphism'.[78]

This is not merely a negative argument—that when we appeal to what is imaginatively credible we must accept these strange irreducible forms of expression as somehow inevitable. The positive side of the argument lies in the kind of imaginative responsiveness which alone can rightly interpret such forms and distinguish between them. It is here that we may find grounds for distinguishing between the convictions of the hero and of the fanatic, and between true and false beliefs. Take Newman's discussion of conscience, for example, in Chapter V of the *Grammar of Assent*. At first glance it may seem to derive from a superseded faculty psychology, and to overlook the fact that he may be speaking merely of the conditioning of our moral responses. The *Notebook*, however, reveals a subtle conception of moral awareness to describe which the terms used—a searcher of hearts, a supreme being obliging—arise 'from the peculiarity of that feeling to which I *give* the name of conscience'. And one moves from this feeling to a conception of a personal God by a great sensitivity to personal relationships and by means of the language used to describe them: 'I have a feeling in my mind, which, as soon as I have occasion to recognise my feeling towards a parent or kind superior I find *interpreted by it*.' But such analogical forms provide a 'key to his perplexity in grasping and defining' only '*when* (a man) has had experience of this world'. Thus conscience is used, not as a term in an argument to prove the existence of God (a procedure plainly contrary to the method and purpose of the *Grammar of Assent*) but as a primary metaphor, drawn from our experience of personal relationships, and acting as an analogue to describe or characterize the nature of our experience of God. Contrasting this with the experience of 'order' (so prominent a feature in arguments for the existence of God), Newman writes: 'Design teaches me power, skill and goodness—not sanctity, not mercy, not a future judgement, which three are the essence of

[78] *N*. ii. 145, 133.

religion'[79]—as they are of the use of the term 'conscience'. Newman's approach but repeats St. Augustine's in the *Confessions*: 'And how shall I find thee, if I remember thee not?'

It is this very complexity of forms and responses that points to an essential distinction: the fanatic is so often the man of *one* idea; illusions do not last. Newman's account of assent reveals the extent to which *all* assents and beliefs raise the question of truth within a complex and not a simple form—a form which belongs essentially to and is inseparable from the very structure of their verification. Like the framework of a George Eliot novel it cannot be by-passed or reduced to a simpler form without changing its character; and it, too, must be lived with to be lived through. But, in religion, what is thus 'dilated'—in the highly charged language of scripture—is 'contracted' into the Creeds. We can never demonstrate *why* this happens or ought to happen; but, by referring to the probable causes in the history of the Church, and particularly in the development of doctrine, what we can do is show *how* it happens. The labyrinthine nature of the problem is revealed when we realize that belief is not only what we move to, but what we start from. Belief is in this latter sense, as Newman remarks, 'a conservative principle of know-ledge'.[80] The fruitful question is not why beliefs are formed, but how we become entitled to the certitude, without which beliefs could neither be formed nor professed. Newman's genius consists in his discovery that not only is a structure of 'probabilities' one of 'growth and production', but that, if we trust it, it enables the movement from assent to certitude, and from faith to belief to take place. In religion, certitude is a 'reward', that is, a gift direct from God.[81]

To talk of aesthetic responses, literary assents, or political commitments is to raise questions of truth in this form, that is, in a mode different from (but not necessarily incompatible

[79] 13 Apr. 1870: *Letters*, xxv. 97.

[80] *GA*, p. 28.

[81] *Letters*, xxi. 270 referring to *Apo.*, pp. 121–3; 291–2 (cp. *GA*, p. 43). Newman's discussion of the distinction between 'human' certainty and the 'certainty of (religious) faith' is tantalizingly condensed. It is similar to Coleridge's distinction (in *BL*, chap. xiii) between primary and secondary imagination, where the latter (literary or 'human' imagination) is the 'echo' of the former (God's 'eternal act of creation'). Newman also seems to take religious certitude as the model for human certitude, arguing that, in each case, God 'has willed us so to act'. In religion, 'He co-operates with us in our acting', bestowing on us 'a certitude which rises higher than the logical force of our conclusions'.

with) questions of logical inference which can be demonstrated to be clearly correct or incorrect. Applied to political assents, this distinction becomes at once obvious. The revolutionary is unmoved by particular questions such as 'what would you put in its place?' because he is affirming a way of life as a whole against which 'nothing counts simply'. What would (and does) count is an adverse experience of *comparable complexity*; and this has to be grown into, as when, for example, the acts of a regime build up and then precipitate the invasion of a Czechoslovakia. Similarly, obstacles to the reform of a religious belief arise from the fact that such forms have acted upon the imagination of the believer as if they were actually perceived by the senses. A believer who was unable to understand the creative role of imagination in perception (but was unconsciously influenced by it) would regard a reform of his belief as effecting a destruction of his perception of the world. His world would have *appeared* to have been destroyed.

To use the model of the arch, as Newman does, is to emphasize this complexity of real assent, and the comparable complexity of its negative, which is called 'loss of faith'. But has the arch a key-stone? If so, then this would be to claim that some one argument or some one event could demonstrate conclusively that the assent was either true or false. Newman's argument, I would suggest, tends against this development of his analogy. He seems to be arguing that the act of real assent, although rational, is not demonstrative: it grows to certitude; and therefore it can be lost only by a comparable process of erosion.[82] There is no crucial instance by which it could be demonstrated to be *simpliciter* true or false.[83]

This and the comparison I have drawn with political assent may enable us to appreciate why Newman is anxious to avoid such simple models for religious assent as the leap of faith, and to prefer more complex ones like the polygon expanding into the enclosing circle. What distinguishes religious from political assent is the even greater degree of the complexity of the con-

---

[82] See Newman's remark that 'A good instance of the difference between imagination and reason is this—that I feel no fear of reading a book like M. Comte's though said to be atheistical, though I *have* an anxiety about looking into Strauss's Life of Christ'. *O* (*T*. p. 46, 4 May 1857).

[83] Cp. D. H. Lawrence's account of the erosion of Will Brangwyn's faith by his wife, Anna, in *The Rainbow*, pp. 173, 202–6.

text. Not only are we obliged to make '*a firm assent* to the word of God *obscurely revealed*'[84], but we seem committed to a devotion and to a fellowship.[85]

When a leap of faith is spoken of, it seems to be interpreted quite arbitrarily. Do we leap straight into the arms of God? What this metaphor can suggest is the decision to abandon one's own subjectivity and accept as true positions held by other people—now and in the past—and accounts about events which happened in the past. It is to acquire a personal depth, which is both collective and historical: it embraces other people's assents as one's own, and it stretches back into time. This effects a personal change; and it is what is qualitatively new: we find ourselves by being in equilibrium with others now and in the past; the polygon of oneself expands into the circle of a world unseen.

The fact that—as the catechism reminds us—what we ask from the Church is faith, shows to what extent religious and political assents are alike. Faith is found in fellowship, in each case a primary condition being that responsiveness to people which, in religion, is to an unseen world as if we saw it. Real assent is always to a 'world'—however diverse or dissociated may be our ways of accounting for it subsequently—and where such a world has ceased to be plausible, the condition for real assent, or, in religion, for the act of faith, may be fatally impaired. We assent to many such 'worlds'—to that of the novelist and dramatist as much as to that of the Gospels and parables.

To the extent to which the novelist or dramatist successfully brings alive the ideas and metaphors which were the cause of his desire to create, so he too creates a world. By his mediation ideas become characters, whose actions coalesce to form a world; and what 'worlds' have in common is their power to

---

[84] *O*, '*Papers on Faith*', 1848 (B.9.11).

[85] *N*. ii. 167, 24 Jan. 1867. '"Catholics do not honestly seek truth". This misapprehension arises from the fact that religion is not solely a *philosophy* (science), but also a *devotion* (passion), and a party adherence or fellowship. Devotion brings in hope and fear—and fellowship brings in fear of scandal. In philosophy there is no fear or consideration of anything but "is this so or not?" but devotion brings in the fear of error and its consequences, and fellowship introduces the necessities of all moving together—the duty of deference to superiors, and consulting for the interest of our neighbours. N.B. *All this must come into my essay on Certitude*' (my italics).

Note how this anticipates the final form of Newman's conception of the Church in the Preface to the third edition of the *Via Media* (London, 1877).

place us under their judgements: they are not where we claim, but where we are claimed. Poets describe them variously as 'spots of time' where, in 'an unattended moment', we are invited to believe—an invitation which comes from outside ourselves, not merely in a spatial sense, but in a temporal one— hence tradition speaks of this world as controlled neither by the present nor by the past, but by 'the gods', which is another way of indicating to what extent religious assent is one in which our experience of time and space undergoes profound modification.

In Newman's elucidating image, it is the difference between seeing a line at first, in its length, sequentially, and then, at right-angles, as a point.[86] We cease to experience simple 'chronology', or past, present, and future as successive stages of ever equal movements, and experience them instead as 'over-lapping and inter-penetrating'.[87] It is, in Eliot's phrase, to move 'in and out of time'. It is to have the capacity both to understand backwards and to live forwards. In religious assent, therefore, in one respect we 'leap'; but in retrospect we experience that leap as precipitated by an accumulation of probabilities; and the difference between Newman and Kierkegaard may well amount to no more than that between retrospective and prospective ways of looking at the same fact: it is spoken of as a 'leap' *before*, and is conceived as a polygon expanding into a circle after. Thus Newman is 'putting the sentiments in order',[88] by trying to understand backwards what has been lived forwards in order to show the conditions which, socially, historically, and reflectively, enable us to be certain that our spontaneous leap of faith is a rational act rather than a merely subjective feeling. Furthermore, if acts of assent are thus a complex of variables, the act of religious assent appears to be the most highly complex; and the theologian will have to be able to detect whether the character claimed for a religious assent is adequately complex, or whether (on the other hand) it has come too easily: it is just as dangerous to believe too little as to believe too much (by requiring an 'excess' of faith, to use

[86] *N.* ii. 165.

[87] F. von Hügel, *Eternal Life*, London, 1912, p. 383.

[88] This is Eliot's distinction also (see below, p. 125). In the *Journals*, Kierkegaard writes: 'Life must be understood backwards. . . . It must be lived forwards' (p. 89). 'Faith is immediacy after reflection' (p. 142).

Newman's expression above).[89] When it is complex, religious assent is not an intuition (or simple assent), but what Newman calls a *contuition*, that is 'a sight of a thing through and by means of the things which lie about it'.[90]

(v) THE SOCIAL FRAMEWORK OF BELIEF

(a) *its pre-conditions*

In Newman's case, this complexity seems to be put at risk by his being a Roman Catholic and thus committed to accepting beliefs upon external authority. How is what appears to be the *imposition* of certitude to be reconciled with Newman's account of its growth? Before dealing with these questions, two points need to be made. First, that doctrinal beliefs are not simply propounded or encountered. They grow out of argument and experience, and are encountered in forms which are already highly developed. Their development, far from being conceived as a chain of linked deductions and inferences in simple systematic form, and as 'a list of articles that can be numbered', is more like a never-ending process of translation and re-translation.

Thus—and this is the second point—beliefs about what has been defined *de fide* are still in growth and remain subject to development. For Newman the role of ecclesiastical authority is to provide an external or negative safeguard against *rudimentary* error—that is all. It is, to this extent, a source of reliable inferences. Newman assumed that 'questions which seemed to be closed are after a course of years re-opened'; and here, he says 'there is a real exercise of private judgment, and an allowable one'.[91] Authority is what preserves development from becoming simple relativism by acting, in the sense later referred to by Matthew Arnold,[92] as an organ of conservation. It provides a social framework for imagination, not an authoritarian substitute.

The development of doctrine, as Newman conceives it, is in fact a prime example of growth in imaginative responsiveness. It requires a determination to turn the mysteries of Revelation

---

[89] See p. 49, above.
[90] *T*, p. 64 (1860?).
[91] In the letter to the Duke of Norfolk (*Difficulties of Anglicans*, ii (1876), 334).
[92] See below, p. 103.

round, until suddenly we discover that they have 'clicked' into our present awareness, itself variable, relative, and changing— but this 'click' or 'focus' will not hold indefinitely, since 'here below to live is to change, and to be perfect is to have changed often'. But although we are always having to change or readjust this focusing, it does not follow that we are committed either to doctrinal relativism, or to 'superficial notions of evolution'. What we are focusing upon will be, in some way unknown to us, always the same datum (or 'deposit'). It is of an 'incomprehensible certainty'.[93] Logically, to talk of approximation is to imply the existence, objectively, of what one is trying to approximate to; and it is in this sense that I would understand what Newman said in the year of his being made a Cardinal— that theology 'makes progress by being always alive to its own fundamental uncertainties'.[94]

This is a claim about the nature of theology which, by bringing him closer to T. S. Eliot, as well as to Péguy and Hopkins, and of course essentially to the Fathers, separates Newman from the Neo-Scholastic tradition. No wonder that he found the scholastics 'cold'; but how right Manning was to see his preference for the Fathers as being a 'literary' one! Newman would certainly have accepted Hopkins's way of stating the distinction as one between 'an equation in theology, the dull algebra of schoolmen', and knowledge 'that leaves their minds swinging, poised but on the quiver . . . the ecstasy of interest'.[95]

But directly the general conception of religious language has ceased to be scholastic and univocal, the most important part of what the Modernists were to ask for has, in practice, been conceded, viz.: the distinction between what is revealed and how it is described, defined, and spoken of.

This has important implications for religion, since, by pre-

---

[93] *Letters of G. M. Hopkins to Robert Bridges*, ed. C. C. Abbott, OUP, 2nd edn., 1955, p. 187, 24 Oct. 1883.

[94] *N.* i. 145; Ward, *Life of Cardinal Newman*, ii. 591; *Letters*, xxix. 118. Cp. Stuart Hampshire on the function of imagination in the development of thought: 'The energy in any imaginative work comes from that destruction of single-mindedness which allows different interpretations at different levels' (*The Morality of Scholarship*, ed. Max Black, New York, 1967, p. 44).

[95] *Letters to Robert Bridges*, p. 188. Two years before, Hopkins had asked Newman if he might bring out a commentary on the *Grammar of Assent*, but Newman had refused, on the grounds that it was superfluous, and 'however brilliant' would 'gain for it a short galvanic life, which has no charms for me' (*Letters*, xxx, 191, 27 Feb. 1883).

supposing a distinction between faith and beliefs, it recognizes
the dilemma experienced by Arnold and Hardy—that we may
be unable to profess our faith. The language of belief, having
become cliché, becomes inadequate to faith; and, unable to
make an adequate profession, we may yet hold what we cannot
or will not explain away, and refuse to deny what we cannot as
yet, reaffirm.[96]

This is the negative implication, the positive is that 'without
formulation there is no interest (and) the clearer the formulation, the greater the interest'.[97] But, since clarity of focus, once
achieved, does not hold indefinitely, we must anticipate, as
necessary and inevitable, new and diverse explanations of our
faith; and it is precisely the present acceptance of plural explanations and theologies which has led to the discovery of
Newman as a major theologian, and, in particular (to quote
Pope Paul), as the theologian of ecumenism and of the dialogue
between Christian and non-Christians. Far from having difficulty in accepting Karl Rahner's contention,[98] for example,
that it is legitimate for Christian theologies to be as various as
the epistemologies on which they are based, Newman strongly
advocated such a diversity of theological interpretations and
schools as the very best protection for the dogmas of faith. He
distinguishes between the Schola—'a generalization for the
decisions of theologians throughout the world'—and 'the
schools of the church', of which it is composed, each of which
has 'a distinct character' of its own, often containing, 'to its
great profit, able men of very different complexions of thought
and of doctrine—as the old Universities did'. Without the
'Schola', 'the dogma of the Church would be the raw flesh
without skin—nay or a tree without leaves—for, as devotional
feelings clothe the dogma on the one hand, so does the teaching
of the Schola on the other.' Security lies in the very density and
diversity of teaching, 'as forming a large body of doctrine which
must be got through before an attack can be made on the
dogma'. The 'serious evil' which now confronts us is our dependence upon the Roman school 'as nearly the only school in the

[96] See pp. 44 and 108.

[97] Hopkins, *Letters to Robert Bridges*, p. 187.

[98] Karl Rahner: 'Pluralism in Theology and the unity of the Church's Profession of
faith', in *Concilium*, June 1969, p. 56.

Church', the other schools having been destroyed by the Revolutions.[99]

Plural theologies require a plurality of theological schools, since the strongest proof is that which rests upon 'supports which are distinct from, or independent of each other'. This is the institutional form of 'saying and unsaying to a positive result', and the means which Christianity requires, if it is to continue to 'modify itself into something that can be believed in'.

(b) *its authority*

Newman's acceptance of ecclesiastical authority (with the reservations and qualifications now to be made) relates to his sense of personal limitation, when he is confronted by the *structure* of Christian Revelation. This can never be interpreted simply as a system of leading ideas, since it is 'neither light nor darkness, but both together. . . . It is not a revealed *system*, but . . . a number of detached and incomplete truths belonging to a vast system unrevealed, of doctrines and injunctions mysteriously connected together . . . '. It is of 'a mystery' and, therefore, of 'a doctrine *lying hid* in language'.[100]

Thus, like Butler before him, Newman believes that why we must hold on to the words and ordinances by which Revelation has come to us is that, apart from them, 'Revelation does not exist, there being nothing else given us by which to ascertain or enter into it'.[101] This is more than the acceptance of language, in distinction from the rationalist (and Cartesian) suspicion of its power to deceive. It is to accept the testimony of a literary culture since, although our efforts may be no better than 'raids upon the inarticulate', Newman, unlike Tyrrell, for example, *trusts* them to succeed. The value of the *Grammar of Assent* for the theologian lies in the soundness of its literary instincts: our conceptions of religious and literary assent are valid explanations to the extent that they are mutually compatible. Newman argues, therefore, that religion cannot maintain its ground without theology, it being both necessary and legitimate to hold

[99] *Letters*, xxii. 98–9, 9 Nov. 1865.
[100] On the Introduction of Rationalistic Principles into Revealed Religion, *ECH* i. 41–2. For the full text and for its publication by T. S. Eliot in *The Criterion*, see below, p. 126.
[101] Ibid., p. 47.

such assertions as that there is one Present and Personal God in two distinct ways—notionally, as a religious proposition, and, empirically, as a statement of a religious fact.[102] Nevertheless, as with T. S. Eliot, so with Newman—the strong sense of his 'shortcomings' before the structure of 'detached and incomplete truths' leads him to assert that we accept as trustworthy what we cannot verify *a priori*: 'we are commanded to believe on authority, instead of holding on proof.'[103] This is what Newman intends by a somewhat condensed passage in the *Apologia*, when he says that the argument about Probability, in matters of religion, became 'an argument from Personality, which in fact is one form of the argument from Authority'. One of the roles of authority in religion is to be the repository of trustworthy testimony: God speaks by the voice of his messengers, whom we trust.[104]

Because faith, however conceived, is a spontaneous act, and because spontaneity—the very power of imagination—presupposes trust, without trust there can be no faith. To allow imagination to diffuse and dissipate where there is initially no acceptance of someone or something as trustworthy, is to risk inevitable disintegration and dissociation. The act of imaginative transformation remains uncompleted; probabilities have failed to converge into certitude; the leap of faith has fallen short. And Icarus dives to his death between two worlds.

Is Newman being too 'trusting'? This is a very strong objection, since it is here that political and sociological considerations may legitimately be introduced. Conditions can arise, socially and politically, which do predispose us to mistrust the testimony of others. And it is not unreasonable to point out that Newman belonged to a class which was brought up to trust, whereas a more general sense of alienation makes such trust nowadays less easy for some, and impossible for others. Furthermore, if we speak of the appeal to conscience or imagination as being, not to a faculty, but to what Coleridge

---

[102] *GA*, p. 91, see above, p. 41.

[103] *Letters*, xxvi. 287.

[104] *Apo.*, p. 121, see the discussion in *Discourses addressed to Mixed Congregations* (1849), 1876, pp. 195–8, and *Gregorianum*, xviii. 219–60: 'Faith—on its human side (not as divine)—is admitting a conclusion on the word of another' (Thesis 10, 11 Jan. 1847, p. 245).

calls 'a testifying state'—that is, to a condition of feeling or sensibility—then this, too, relies upon and presupposes a social formation (as Newman admits in the *Grammar of Assent*).[105] Even so, the general question remains untouched: can we live without trusting, or without spontaneity. Of course, we can be alienated and psychically damaged, but (mental illness on one side) we are merely bringing into the argument questions about the strength and quality of response, not objections to the response itself. To say that we cannot now be as trusting as Newman is not, logically, to refute the assertion that 'to act you must assume, and that assumption is faith'. But it is to make a legitimate objection, which must be considered in the next section.

In religion, we trust in order to act; and in order to define the function of authority in religion, it is necessary to decide to whom that authority is primarily addressed. Newman argues that it is not, in the first instance, addressed to philosophers, since 'Revelation was not given us to satisfy doubts, but to make us better men.'[106] The purpose of the guarantee that the Church as a whole (as it is expressed through the Pope, the Bishops in Council, or the *consensus fidelium*) cannot err in believing is to trust that it cannot be misled.[107] About what? The answer is, surely, the faith that we must *put into practice*.[108] It is the function of Popes and Bishops to preach this duty to the people; or, in Newman's words, the moral law is their *raison d'être*. By this is meant that their authority, far from overriding conscience, is derived from it, since, ultimately, it is directed to securing our union with God in *conscientious* and prayerful obedience. Authority's claim not to mislead is, as I have suggested, directed primarily, not at philosophical speculation, but at those teachings which, as they are applied, are the grounds of our union with God. And it is significant that *Lumen Gentium*, for example, specifically denies that there can be any new public revelation pertaining to the divine deposit of the faith.[109]

However whole-heartedly and imaginatively we assent to the

[105] *GA*, p. 83.
[106] *PPS* i. 229.
[107] *Lumen Gentium* ii. 12 (in *Documents of Vatican II*, ed. Abbott, 1966.)
[108] Ibid., iii. 25. (see James 2:18)
[109] Ibid., iii. 25.

mysterious language of scripture, the question remains—what are we to believe? The knowledge we have gained remains ambiguous and empirically unverified. It is incomplete. It finds its completion, according to Newman, in action.[110] But such completion is social: religious explanation and act cohere within a community of acts (or in what Newman calls a 'polity').

Life may be too short for a religion of inferences, but it is long enough for us to verify our paraphrases (or 'notions') of the inherited language of the Bible and the Church in the living of them. And it is this element of *praxis*, socially conceived, which gives us the clue to why Newman's conception of authority, although necessary, is so carefully qualified. It also explains more fully how Newman conceives the movement from imagination to belief, and in what circumstances it takes place. To paraphrase Coleridge,[111] faith and belief are not diverse things but the same thing in different periods of its growth. The inherited language of faith, to which we make an imaginative assent, and from which our convictions arise, is of an uncompromisingly symbolic character: it is a many-faced challenge which never yields a final paraphrase: in fact its linguistic mode seems deliberately chosen thus to preserve it for infinite use by all generations. But it is more than a highly complex and ambiguous set of words 'thrown out' at what it cannot fully encompass: it is language about realities which require us to act, and in acting to verify the truth (and reality) of what is asserted: 'Faith is a *firm assent* to the word of God *obscurely revealed.*'[112]

III. The Modernist Dilemma Anticipated

If our convictions are authenticated by actions which take place within a community of acts, what is presupposed is a community of a very different kind from the Church as conventionally envisaged; and it is not for nothing that Newman's life and

---

[110] *GA*, p. 91: 'Knowledge must ever precede the exercise of the affections.' But, at the same time, 'by trying we make proof; by doing we come to know' (*PPS*. viii. 113), and 'that a thing is true, is no reason that it should be said, but that it should be done' (*PPS* v. 45).

[111] See above, p. 11.

[112] 'Papers on Faith', 1848, *O* (B.9.11).

writings strike one as being so especially concerned with the theology of community. In his conception of the Oratory, as much as in his idea of a University, he is concerned to bring out the principles which, creative of an authenticating way of life, enable our beliefs, actions, and prayer to exist in a life-giving equilibrium; and, since 'to live is to change', this equilibrium succeeds in perpetuating its identity by its power to develop into what can continue to be believed in.[113] What Newman is opposed to is what he found when he became a Roman Catholic—a community standing off defensively from a changing world, and alienating its members, by hesitating on the margins, and so confusing essential distinctions as to imply that beliefs might be imposed independently of our experience of faith.[114] This was the attitude which precipitated the crisis of 1870, when the definition of papal infallibility was promulgated in a church unprepared for it. Such attitudes were rooted in a conception of the supernatural as being, not only self-sufficient, but even more immediately 'real' than the natural order.[115] What is then over-emphasized is God's 'apartness', in distinction from his presence, 'not alongside of creatures, but behind them, as the light which shines through a crystal and lends it whatever lustre it may have'.[116] These words are von Hügel's when faced, like Newman, with another and later crisis of authority within the Church—that of 'Modernism'. For both men, God was to be 'loved here, not apart from (his creatures), but through and in them'; and a healthy spiritual life required the practice of 'the outgoing movement towards Multiplicity and Contingency'. In other words, to be made by religion is to participate in the 'great sacred organisms of the Family, Society, and the Church'.[117]

But to hold so highly a participative conception of personal fulfilment within an institutional church seems at odds with the persistent behaviour of the institution which, in the words of George Tyrrell, was like a train, with the Pope as the engine

---

[113] The phrase is Eliot's, see below, p. 111, and see also the Chapter Address for 1 Feb. 1878, in Placid Murray, *Newman the Oratorian*, Dublin, 1969.

[114] Cp. George Tyrrell's criticism of a theology 'which draws ideas from ideas'.

[115] See Manning's *Eternal Priesthood*, 17th edn., 1907, p. 98, where he writes: 'The invisible world is the substance, the visible world but the shadow. To minds that are not supernatural this world, loud and glaring, is palpable, and therefore thought to be real.'

[116] F. von Hügel, *The Mystical Element of Religion*, 1923, ii. 353.

[117] Ibid., ii. 353, 356, 365.

driver and the laity as the passengers. Such were the circumstances which, in the early years of the twentieth century,
obliged von Hügel and his fellow 'modernists', as they had
obliged Newman in 1870, to oppose those who wished
to concentrate the Church upon the papacy at the expense of
its prophetical and theological function.[118] It was not the
Modernists but Newman who referred to the 'Nihilism in the
Catholic body', whose rulers 'forbid, but they do not direct or
create'. In such circumstances to believe was to obey, and for
a theologian or a layman to show initiative or to use his
imagination was for him to be already 'on the road to perdition'.

What Modernism did was to raise fundamental questions in
a new form. It anticipated a shift from the deductive imposition
of beliefs to their elucidation, *inductively*, as they arise from the
questions posed by faith. If, now, we accept authority only with
such reservations, what authorizes a present claim to believe?

The answer is what it always was. We allow our imaginative
assents to be brought into accord with trustworthy testimony
and reliable inferences. It is this accord which gives substance
to the metaphors, symbols, and stories which are the primary
forms of faith. As I have argued, such forms have life in proportion to their substance or 'density', and this density in, for
example, Shakespeare and the Metaphysical poets, is at once
religious, intellectual, and social. Even Strauss in his *Life of Jesus*
is not prepared to reduce 'myths' to mere stories. They are
'fictions, (which) having met with faith, come to be *received*
among the legends of a people'.[119]

It is within this highly qualified and restricted sense of external testimony, which is socially trustworthy and rationally
plausible, that Newman conceives 'authority'. It is not a substitute for imagination. It possesses, not inspiration, but infallibility, which Newman conceives negatively, as an external help
only: 'No promise of inspiration is given to the Church, but of
infallibility, which is not a habit or permanent faculty, but
consists in an *external* divine protection, when the Church

---

[118] Newman's conception of the Church as performing the offices of Christ as
Prophet, Priest, and King, and its adaptation by von Hügel are discussed in my *Newman
and the Common Tradition*, chap. X. For the importance Newman attached to this
conception for 'my essay on Certitude' see above, p. 70 and *N*. ii. 167.

[119] D. F. Strauss, *Life of Jesus* (1835–6), London, 1974, p. 86 (my italics).

speaks *ex cathedra*, against her falling into error.'[120]

Apropos of the events of 1870, Newman writes 'the very idea of infallibility is a negative'.[121] The definition of papal infallibility is likely, in effect, to restrict rather than to increase the Pope's power: 'hitherto he has done what he would, because its limits were not defined—now he must act by rule.'[122] True to the principles I have described, Newman trusted in the slow, assimilative power of 'the general Catholic intelligence (where) the ultimate decision rests': 'No abstract definition can determine particular fact.'[123]

Given time, therefore, a second council would set right the work half-finished by the first; and this is what has happened. What has also happened is that the Church as a whole has paid the price for its authoritarian misconceptions as it has moved inexorably towards the margins. Its failure to provide the communities in which imaginative convictions could be authenticated is not simply a theological failure. It continues the process begun at the Reformation of weakening what Newman calls the *external* evidence of religion: 'accordingly, Revealed Religion was in great measure stripped of its proof'[124] or, as we should now say, of the empirical means of its verification. The existence of a healthy, sanctifying, and united community is referred to by Newman as '*the* argument, inattention to which, makes the metaphysical and historical arguments of unbelief overcome the mind'.[125]

Similarly, a Church which does not care to be socially plausible, in a changing industrial society, soon moves to the margins; and a God become implausible both to its rationality and to its literary imagination remains credible only to children, visionaries, and professional theologians, whose concep-

---

[120] *The Via Media of the Anglican Church*, London, 1877, i. 310 (my italics). It is interesting that this remark appears as a footnote added in 1877 to a discussion by Newman while still an Anglican on the promises of inspiration made to the Apostles in scripture. I am indebted to Mgr. M. Nédoncelle for pointing out to me that, after Vatican I, Newman may have wished to modify or restrict his former position (see also Maurice Nédoncelle, *Le Chrétien appartient à deux mondes*, Editions du Centurion, 1970, p. 173 and note).

[121] 3 Apr. 1871. *Letters*, xxv. 309.

[122] Ibid., p. 204.

[123] Ibid., p. 71.

[124] *OUS*, p. 69.

[125] *O (T*, p. 49).

tions by being thus 'unlettered' are starved into 'notions' and languish in seminary confinement. Once the connections between the primary forms of faith (its metaphors and symbols) and the beliefs they are held to have entailed are loosened, the language of religion ceases to nourish the hitherto common language of church and society. As religious words and expressions fall out of general use, so the secular sentiments they stand for fade with them, and a common grammar is thought no longer to exist. The language of belief is then felt as an alien rhetoric without power to affect social and political actions; and the consequences envisaged by Newman in 1870 then come to pass. Looking beyond 'the Church', he foresaw a society in which 'the lowest class, which is most numerous, and is infidel, will rise up from the depths of the modern cities, and will be the new scourges of God'.[126]

Here are the circumstances, historically, which make for a much more radical 'great divide' than that between us and the Reformation or the seventeenth century. They predispose us to accept a distinction between our faith *in* the reality disclosed by imagination, and our belief *that* the meanings traditionally entailed are true. Can we continue, in Newman's way, to hold beliefs which we can neither prove nor explain? Or have we now to go beyond Newman and press the distinction, in religion, between faith and belief and, in literature, between poetry and belief? Is there now, as the Modernists assumed, a radical and seemingly unbridgeable divide between, on the one hand, the metaphorical and symbolic language of imagination and faith and, on the other, the language of belief and conceptual formulation? Have the questions changed so radically as to invalidate Newman's grammar of imagination and belief?

Appendix: Newman on *Imaginative* Assent

In the archives of Birmingham Oratory (A.30.11) and headed 'Chapter iii para. 1. On apprehension and assent through the imagination considered in reference to the being of a God'.

A study of the manuscript sources of the early drafts of the substance of the *Grammar of Assent* shows that Newman's original distinction was between notional and *imaginative* assent. This is

<hr>

126 *Letters*, xxv. 337.

established by the manuscript headed 'Chapter iii para 1', which was worked and reworked on at least three occasions, 26–8 April, 5 May, and 7 September (and in another manuscript copy on 15 July) 1868.

The relevant part of Newman's argument is as follows:

5. The apprehension, which is thus a condition of assent to a proposition, is of two kinds, apprehension of its meaning and of its object; the former of these is mainly an act of pure intellect, the latter an act of experience, present or past, and of memory in aid of experience; and according, and so far as, the apprehension is of the former or the latter kind, so is the assent languid or energetic.

The next paragraph (6) is much amended, and it is the first draft which is, for our purposes, the most significant. In the following copy the amendments are printed in the line above:

taken to stand

6. –If [by] the faculty of imagination be understood
    not for an inventive power   for
  –the power, not only of invention, but of the power

  –which attends upon memory of recalling to the mind
while
  –and making present the absent, then the former
fitly   notional
  –kind of apprehension may be called intellectual,

  –the latter may be called by way of contrast

  –imaginative.

From the first draft we can see that Newman's original conception of imagination is purely Coleridgean: it is the inventive (or 'essemplastic') power. The final paragraph summarizes the implications of the distinction thus:

7. According as the apprehension is notional or imaginative, so may the assent be called one or the other, the notional assent being languid, and the imaginative energetic. At the same time, though there are two kinds of apprehension, there are not two kinds of assent: but in both cases it is one and the same assent in its nature given to different subject matters, in one case to notions, in the other to imaginations.

PART TWO

RELIGIOUS IMAGINATION IN THE NINETEENTH CENTURY AND AFTER

3

The Changing of the Questions

I. Between Two Worlds

(1) THE REAL DIVIDE?

The nineteenth century has to face the assumption, first suggested by Feuerbach and then promulgated by Marx, that to persist in religious belief may be a sign of a malfunctioning or 'alienated' sensibility. The metaphors by which such writers as Lancelot Andrewes and George Herbert had expressed (and felt) their beliefs 'as immediately as the odour of a rose' are first tolerated and then dismissed as subjective 'projections'. The overlap of religion and literature is no longer assumed to be *sui generis* but is held to be an accident of cultural history. Is it still true that 'a great poet must be, *implicitè* if not *explicitè*, a profound Metaphysician'?[1] Or is Eliot right in saying that the poet brings us 'to a condition of serenity, stillness, and reconciliation' only to be obliged to leave us 'as Virgil left Dante, to proceed towards a region where that guide can avail us no farther'?[2]

This is what is now in question. Poetic faith and religious belief tend to represent distinct and dissociated starting-points. Theoretically, literary faith is negatively conceived as a suspension of disbelief, while religion has become de-mythologized into notions, articles of belief, and legal maxims. Until the later nineteenth century, however, it was still possible to take the overlap of religion and literature largely for granted. They were part of a common literary culture, and still shared a common grammar.[3] Culture and religion, belief and imagination, criti-

[1] Coleridge, Letter to Sotheby, 13 July 1802 in *Collected Letters of Samuel Taylor Coleridge*, E. L. Griggs, Oxford, 1956–71, ii. 810; see also *The Friend*, vol. iii, Essay VII: 'From Shakspeare to Plato, from the philosophic poet to the poetic philosopher, the transition is easy.'

[2] *OPP*, p. 87.

[3] I use 'grammar' to refer to that underlying form, or structure, which we discover as we learn and use a language. When this is both adequate to our needs as specialists (whether as theologians, poets, statesmen, or psychiatrists), and yet intelligible to us as common readers, we may speak of a common grammar, and of its acting as a bridge between us and our specialist disciplines.

cism and theology are *felt* to be one, and therefore different ways of saying the same thing. They face common problems: that of maintaining continuity—in literature with moral values, and in religion with its sources in scripture and tradition. In each case what is presupposed is a living past continuously available to the present. But can this continuity and availability be taken for granted in an environment which, year by year, becomes relentlessly different from that in which such beliefs and expectations originated?

In his inaugural lecture at Cambridge,[4] C. S. Lewis remarks that if there is a great divide in human experience it is not between medieval and modern, but between pre-industrial and industrial—'between Jane Austen and us comes the birth of the machines'. A change occurs in the environment so radical as to produce a shift in consciousness. In the words of Disraeli, industrialization has split England into two nations—the rich and the poor—and 'there is no community in England', only aggregation; 'but aggregation under circumstances which make it rather a dissociating than a uniting principle'.[5] This is the England of Wodgate, of Dickens' Coketown in *Hard Times*— that no-man's-land of hard fact and dreary uniformity, whose only mystery is who belongs to the eighteen denominations which compose its religious life. In Arnold, too, it is the city— with its heart-wearying roar—which symbolizes a unique process of dissociation. Yet for him, as for his contemporaries, this is a process which is still, in certain respects, reversible: we can revert to, or still bring about under new conditions, an *organic* society—that is, one which accepts a responsibility to embody values, which we learn as we fulfil the duties of a particular role or station. The options remain open—even for Mill.

For him, they are characterized by Bentham and Coleridge. The former takes his stand outside received opinions, language, and institutions; the latter within them. Bentham asks—are they true? Coleridge asks—what is the truth they have preserved? Each has almost equal power to convince; yet taken in isolation from the other, Coleridge cannot leave the Church, and Bentham ends in Coketown. Neither alternative is

---

[4] *De Descriptione Temporum*, 1954, reprinted in *They asked for a Paper*, London, 1962, pp. 9–25.

[5] *Sybil*, chap. 5.

acceptable. Yet although the habit of analysis and the unrelenting pursuit of social reform wears away the culture of the feelings, Mill believes the process to be reversible. As he affirms in his *Autobiography*, at the end of the struggle for social betterment lies the reward of a resumption of the 'perennial sources of happiness'—the Wordsworthian vision of nature.[6]

In the early years of the Industrial Revolution it still seemed plausible to seek for the antidote to the mechanistic view of the world, and its application by capitalism to social and industrial life, in a simple revival of past forms. The experience did not yet seem to be irreversible. Hence what is called the Gothic revival—'Gothic', because it was believed that in medieval forms the peculiar integrity of the Christian response to society was to be located. It can be argued that all religions, and the Christian religion in particular, commit their believers to some kind of 'organic' or sacramental conception of society. Christians are bidden to realize their beliefs in terms of their membership one of another; and since that membership is talked of in metaphors of the Body of Christ, then an expectation arises that the forms and structures of society are themselves alive—or can be made so. If this is so, then the post-medieval development of a society based upon new principles of financial and technological mechanism is bound to constitute a continuing challenge to such religious beliefs and their associated metaphysical presuppositions. These changes are still interpreted as 'putting an end to all feudal, patriarchal, idyllic relations', or as bringing in a new age of 'sophisters, economists, and calculators'. Of the preceding quotations, the first is from Marx, the second from Burke; but when 'the hardships of life' come by chance and with injustice, all seem to agree that 'it kills a man's love for his country', or, in other words, that a past moral order has been violated. What Marx, Burke, and Coleridge also have in common is their vision of the alternative society as one in which, when sawing down a tree, 'we shall discuss metaphysics, criticise poetry when hunting a buffalo, and write sonnets while following the plough'. This could be Marx in *The German Ideology*: it is in fact Southey in 1794. Some fifty years later, the youthful Marx and Engels had a similar vision—of the com-

[6] J. S. Mill, *Autobiography*, Oxford, 1949, chap. V, p. 125. See also Mill's essays on Bentham and Coleridge.

munist society, where it is 'possible for me to do one thing today and another tomorrow, to hunt in the morning, fish in the afternoon, rear cattle in the evening, criticise after dinner, just as I have a mind, without ever becoming hunter, fisherman, shepherd, or critic'.[7]

The vision of Pantisocracy was not confined to the Left Bank of Susquehanna; but where the 'medievalists' differed from Marx was in the extent to which they failed to recognize the uniqueness of the process which had occasioned the changes they lamented, and its apparently irreversible nature. Instead, they sought for a simple 'home-coming' to the past. Yet without this framework of medieval or Gothic analogues—call it what we will—it is difficult to see how values could have been perpetuated—how without the Gothic chrysalis the socialist gadfly could have been born. The age of chivalry may be dead, but its conception of 'largesse', or public wealth, has never been more necessary. One does not easily turn one's back on Ruskin's remark that an employer is just only if he deals with a subordinate 'as he would with his own son'. And his conclusion 'that such paternalism is a mirror of the basic paternalism of the natural order' presses the question to what extent Christianity, with its talk of a Father and of the Body of Christ, is not, of its very nature, always committed to some kind of *organic* hope or intention for society.

But how, in a society which seeks to become and to remain politically plural, ethically permissive, and metaphysically uncommitted can we remain within a tradition which appears to have been so thoroughly superseded, or hold beliefs which were formed before the 'great divide'? To what extent do the truth-claims of a religion depend upon their continuing to find convincing ground or acceptance in a culture radically distinct from that within which they were formed?

(II) THE POLAR METAPHOR

As far back as 1820 Coleridge had identified this problem, describing it in the form of a contest between 'the two great moving principles of social humanity: religious adherence to the past . . . the desire and the admiration of permanence . . .; and

---

[7] *The German Ideology*, in Karl Marx and Friedrich Engels, *Basic Writings*, ed. L. S. Feuer, London, Fontana, 1969, p. 295.

the passion for increase of knowledge, the mighty instincts of *progression* and *free agency*'.[8] 150 years later, the Soviet poet Yevtuschenko, himself a citizen of a society which claims, by means of a successful revolution, to have accomplished a successful *transition*, writes

> I live only as I
> Let my nerves be strained
>   like the wires
> between the city of No
>   and the city of Yes.

What is chiefly interesting about this polar metaphor is its persistence. It is not a metaphor of revolutionary 'transition'; and I shall argue that neither the metaphor of simple 'transition' nor that of 'holding fast' to inherited values and beliefs is adequate to the choices offered by 'the change of consciousness' effected by an industrial society. What is as much responsible as any other factor for our failure to recognize the alternatives for what they are is the continuing divorce of religion from imagination; and what chiefly contributed to this failure was the determination throughout the nineteenth century to identify certain persistent forms of religious imagination with simple 'loss of faith'.

Although the self-confidence of a Coleridge or Newman may end in the despair of an Arnold or Hardy, what is common is the continuing acceptance that the weight of the past must be borne and explained: intellectually it may grow increasingly inaccessible, but the strength of our sympathy does not diminish. Its power over us is legitimate, but mysterious; it is a mystery which has to be understood. In the words of George Eliot, if our well-regulated minds 'sigh for the departed shades of vulgar errors', it is because 'the loves and sanctities of our life' have 'deep immovable roots in memory'. If they have not, then Heaven knows where our social and intellectual striving might lead us.

It is this way in which the past is accepted which characterizes the literature of the period as being uniquely on the border between belief and unbelief; and it is for this reason that the persistence of the polar metaphor assumes great significance.

[8] *Table Talk and Omniana*, Oxford, 1917, pp. 416–17.

Its form presupposes some kind of connection between past and present—but of what kind? Is it of an irresolvable duality?

The problem finds it focus in the questions about Jesus which are raised, for example, by Strauss's *Life of Jesus*. The historical acceptance of Christianity establishes it as a true myth, but since, therefore, it is a narrative 'which thus speaks of imagination as reality', what are the facts to which it points, and how is it true? If Jesus was not the Incarnate son of God, who was he? What actually happened?

These are the questions which prompted so many nine-teenth-century writers to produce their own Lives of Jesus. Even Coleridge toyed with the notion: 'I have since my twentieth year meditated on an heroic poem on the siege of Jerusalem by Titus—this is the pride and stronghold of my hope.' In the end, however, he came down on the side of traditional belief. Browning, on the other hand, concluded that St. John invented facts he did not experience in order to en-courage belief in the values Jesus stood for. Only through a false fact could posterity believe they saw the star John saw:

> —ye needs must apprehend what truth
> I see, reduced to plain historic fact,
> Diminished into clearness, proved a point
> And far away.

George Eliot, as if paraphrasing this passage, wrote:

It seems to me the soul of Christianity lies not at all in the facts of an individual life, but in the ideas of which that life was the meeting-point and the new starting-point.

She, too, like Renan, remained preoccupied with the person of Jesus, as witness her treatment of Daniel Deronda; but throughout her novels there remains the seemingly unresolved contradiction—that although Christianity cannot be a saving fact, it may be a saving lie. This had been Feuerbach's position. It was to become George Eliot's.

(III) GEORGE ELIOT'S USE OF THE FEUERBACHIAN FRAMEWORK

It is Ludwig Feuerbach who, in Marx's words, 'resolves the religous essence into the *human* essence' and thus reduces religion to its secular basis: 'the earthly family is discovered to be the secret of the holy family.'[9] Feuerbach's *The Essence of Christianity* was first published in 1841 and translated into English by George Eliot in 1854. Its argument is that religion is the first form of self-consciousness, being the child-like condition of humanity. It precedes philosophy, as feeling precedes rational reflection. Thus it is a process of projection, yet man has to discover his nature as projected before he can identify it. We must first invest our feelings with anthropomorphic forms before we can recognize them for what they are in themselves: 'Thus what theology and philosophy have held to be God . . . is not God, but that which they have held not to be God is God: namely, the attribute, the quality, whatever has reality. Hence he alone is the true atheist to whom the predicates of the Divine Being—for example, love, wisdom, justice—are nothing; not he to whom merely the subject of these predicates is nothing.'[10] The value of religious descriptions is, therefore, that they are therapeutic: they help us to recognize our natures and their personal limitations. Safely de-mythologized and reduced to clear conceptions, they help us into ethical reality. Unconsciously persisted in they foster wish-fulfilment and moral illusions. Marx wished to go further: religion is what alienates man from himself by perverting his consciousness. Its very existence is indicative of a 'self-cleavage and self-contradictoriness' of the secular basis. To recommend it is to recommend an opiate. Feuerbach merely interpreted the world: 'the point, however, is to *change* it.' The projections can be de-mythologized and fully resolved by revolutionary social change.

Although Feuerbach held that 'Religion is the disuniting of man from himself' because it sets 'God before him as the antithesis of himself', he did not wish to banish religious belief, only to transcend it, since it was an essential transitional or mediating structure:

God in the sense of a *nomen proprium*, not of a vague, metaphysical entity, is essentially an object only of religion, not of philosophy,—of feeling, not of the intellect—of the heart's necessity, not of the mind's freedom: in short, an object which is the reflex not of the theoretical but of the practical tendency in man.[11]

[9]Marx, *Theses on Feuerbach*, iv, vi.
[10] Op. cit., Harper Torchbooks edn., 1957, p. 21.
[11] Op. cit., pp. 33, 186.

This, too, was the position of his translator, the novelist George Eliot. Feuerbach's reduction of theology to anthropology informs her novels, but it is responsible for the depth of her compassion as well as for her understanding of the rightful importance of religion in the lives of the simple people who compose the world of *Adam Bede*: the sophisticated reader may see in Methodism 'nothing more than low-pitched gables up dingy streets, sleek grocers, sponging preachers, and hypocritical jargon', whereas George Eliot sees a Methodist meeting as one where 'a crowd of rough men and weary-hearted women drank in a faith which was a rudimentary culture, which linked their thoughts with the past, lifted their imagination above the sordid details of their own narrow lives, and suffused their souls with the sense of a pitying, loving, infinite Presence, sweet as summer to the houseless needy'.[12] The Feuerbachian note here is obvious; but there is also a Marxian intimation in what Dinah says later in the novel:

> But I've noticed, that in these villages where the people lead a quiet life among the green pastures and the still waters, tilling the ground and tending the cattle, there's a strange deadness to the Word, as different as can be from the great towns like Leeds, where I once went to visit a holy woman who preaches there. It's wonderful how rich is the harvest of souls up those high-walled streets, where you seemed to walk as in a prison yard, and the ear is deafened with the sounds of worldly toil.[13]

What do Feuerbach and George Eliot mean by their use of 'sacred' and 'religious'?[14] In distinction from Marx, they each retain a religious framework for their world by holding their judgement of its truth or falsity in suspense, since by conceding 'to belief at least an historical validity', unbelief (and belief) gain what George Eliot translates as 'breathing space'.[15] By

---

[12] *Adam Bede*, Everyman edn., 1960, p. 38.

[13] *Adam Bede*, p. 91.

[14] For Feuerbach moral relations are 'per se religious' (op. cit., p. 271), marriage is 'sacred in itself', and eating and drinking is, 'in fact, in itself a religious act' (p. 277). In her Journals, George Eliot speaks of the 'sacred past', and of Esther's relation to Felix Holt as 'the first religious experience of her life'. Of the illusions of Esther's father, the Revd Rufus Lyon, she writes: 'For what we call illusions are often, in truth, a wider vision of past and present realities'. (*Felix Holt*, chap. XVI). A major part of George Eliot's intention is, as a novelist, to explore such questions in terms of the personal relationships which form the novel.

[15] Feuerbach, op. cit., p. 192.

using religious 'projections' as guides to life, she is enabled to name those experiences—of love, duty, and retributive justice—which, though real and abiding, reveal their true meaning only through use: we must live with them to live through them. George Eliot speaks freely of God, therefore, and of the 'divine mystery'; although (unlike Dostoevsky), when she does so, there is no sharp alteration of focus. However, this use of what might be called the Feuerbachian framework is a source of much imaginative originality. It loosens, while it retains, the connection between what people say they believe and what reality drives them to do; it provides the poles of the ironic interplay; it establishes the gap between aspiration and fulfilment. In *Middlemarch* it is responsible for her compassionate understanding of the religious 'projections' of Bulstrode, and for the inevitably tragic relation between Rosamond—the Middlemarch beauty who is determined not to marry a Middlemarcher—and Lydgate—the innovating outsider. Each 'projects' irredeemably upon the other. But it is always the characters thus *negatively* conceived who are the most convincing: the spiritual development of a Dorothea and the affirmations of a Will Ladislaw are less sharply focused and realized: they are imaginatively inadequate to the aspirations of such 'ardently willing souls' and 'finely touched spirits'—to such new forms of consciousness.

In theory, the mystery of human motivation is temporary and reducible to determining causes. George Eliot adopts Mill's image of the great web which, in theory, is knowable, but, in practice, is not; yet once we become able to know sufficient of the relation of causes to effects our behaviour can be rationally calculated to achieve its proper ends. Such a world is most convincingly grasped in its *negative* instances, where behaviour which is the result of obvious defects demonstrates the iron law of consequences. It is less convincing when dealing positively with the ardent aspirations of a Dorothea's love or with Maggie Tulliver's sense of duty and its renunciation. This is the mystery we cannot as yet resolve; yet the safest course is to conceive that 'the will of God is the same thing as the will of other men' to which we should therefore conform.[16] This is essentially a

---

[16] J. W. Cross, *George Eliot's Life*, 1885, p. 427.

conservative position, in which 'conformity' is more prudent that 'nonconformity',[17] so if you lose your culture, you lose your religious conditioning. It is not proof against radical change. Until the parousia George Eliot remains suspended between a dying world whose beliefs must be grown into in order to be grown out of, and a world (or web) as yet unrevealed of intelligible and calculable causes. The words God, Immortality, Duty—'pronounced with terrible earnestness'— remain unresolved.

II. Varieties of Modernism

(IV) MATTHEW ARNOLD

> What today is atheism, tomorrow will be religion.
>
> LUDWIG FEUERBACH

A further factor in what appears to be a unique and irreversible change of consciousness is that, as the environment is transformed by industry, the pastoral sources of traditional religious imagery seem not only outmoded but invalidated. Christianity disappears first from the rational life of man, and then from his environment. In Feuerbach's words: 'it is nothing more than a fixed idea that stands in most glaring contradiction to our fire and life-insurance companies, our railroads and steam engines, our picture galleries, our military and industrial schools, our theatres and scientific museums.'[18]

Since a god that is dead to reason soon disappears from the environment of an industrial society, are there any grounds remaining by reference to which talk about God remains plausible? Matthew Arnold answers this question by appealing to 'all that host of allies which Wordsworth includes under the one name of *imagination*'. Talk about God therefore can still remain plausible to the literary imagination, and the work which remains to be effected is 'of again cementing the alliance between the imagination and conduct'.[19] This is how we should understand Arnold's celebrated dictum on the relation of poetry to religion:

The future of poetry is immense, because in poetry, where it is

[17] Ibid., p. 517.
[18] Op. cit., p. xix.
[19] M. Arnold, *God and the Bible*, 1875, p. xiii.

worthy of its high destinies, our race, as time goes on, will find an ever surer and surer stay. There is not a creed which is not shaken, not an accredited dogma which is not shown to be questionable, not a received tradition which does not threaten to dissolve. Our religion has materialised itself in the fact, in the supposed fact; it has attached its emotion to the fact, and now the fact is failing it. But for poetry the idea is everything; the rest is a world of illusion, of divine illusion. Poetry attaches its emotion to the idea; the idea *is* the fact. The strongest part of our religion today is its unconscious poetry.[20]

This was written by Matthew Arnold over a hundred years ago, in 1880. The conclusion is frequently misunderstood: it does not assert that religion should become poetry by evaporating, as it were, into figures of speech (although this meaning can be drawn from Arnold's theological writings). What is asserted here is that a religion that turns its back on poetry and the imagination is under sentence of death, since it is peculiarly within the experiences it shares with poetry and literature that religion lives most characteristically.

Why this remains a *locus classicus* is that our discussions about religious statements—whether they are true or false, and are about facts or emotions—do not seem to have advanced substantially beyond Arnold. Even his contradictions remain ours. Striving to separate himself from what he conceived to be the dead forms and wrong assumptions of what we now call institutionalized religion and he called the Church of England, Arnold is driven to talk not of God but of 'the eternal, not ourselves, which makes for righteousness', not of religion but of 'morality touched by emotion'. Such expressions invite the attention of philosophers, and Arnold was thought to have been refuted by F. H. Bradley in a satirical passage in *Ethical Studies*:[21]

'Is there a God?' asks the reader. 'Oh yes', replies Mr Arnold, 'and I can verify him in experience.' 'And what is he then?' cries the reader. 'Be virtuous, and as a rule you will be happy', is the answer. 'Well, and God?' 'That is God'; says Mr Arnold; 'there is no deception, and what more do you want?' I suppose we do want a good deal more. Most of us, certainly the public Mr Arnold addresses, want something they can worship; and they will not find that in an hypostasized copy-book heading. . . .

[20] *Essays in Criticism*, 1888, second series, 'The Study of Poetry'.
[21] Oxford, 1927, p. 318, n. 2.

Bradley has simple fun with 'the eternal not ourselves which makes for cleanliness': whether you call it 'clap-trap', as he does, depends upon your sense of humour. Nowadays our darker and sicker sense of humour might find Bradley's attempt to resolve the dilemma equally rhetorical. The dilemma remains: it obstinately refuses to be dispersed. And Arnold's continuing importance is that he never gives up; and the remarks he throws out are as useful to us now as when they were written: 'It is not hard to know God, provided one will not force oneself to define him. . . . Religion is neither a theology nor a theosophy; it is more than all this.' In one of his last theological works, *God and the Bible*,[22] he dismisses as 'ridiculous' the attempts by some philosophers 'to seek to discard the name of *God* and to substitute for it such a name as the *Unknowable*', arguing that the former is a positive name (which has so engaged all men's feelings) and that the latter 'is a name merely negative. And no man could ever have cared anything about God in so far as he is simply unknowable. "The unknowable is our refuge and strength, a very present help in trouble" is what would occur to no man to think or say.' Here the poet replies effectively to the philosopher. He is securing the truth as he experiences it from further verbal invasions or reductions—even when, as in Arnold's case, the poet seems caught out in a contradiction. If we should not discard the name of God why, elsewhere, does he speak of the eternal not-ourselves?

Arnold holds that we anthropomorphize our religious experience, and that the form this anthropomorphism (or what he calls *aberglaube*) takes is for our religious language to become an unconscious reflection of our social, even economic, language. Thus the 'heavy-handed Protestant Philistine'—'sincere, gross of perception, prosaic'—sees in 'Paul's mystical idea of man's investiture with the righteousness of God nothing but a strict legal transaction',[23] and the documents of the Westminster Assembly (1643) are referred to dismissively as 'a machinery of covenants, conditions, bargains, and parties-contractors, such as could have proceeded from no one but the born Anglo-Saxon man of business, British or American'.[24] The conclusion to

[22] London, 1875, p. xlv.
[23] *St. Paul and Protestantism*, London, 1870, p. 116.
[24] Ibid, p. 19.

which Arnold is leading is that our contemporary understanding of religion can be divorced neither from its social context in the past, nor from our experience of that context in the present—as dead, and therefore no longer operative.

In such circumstances Arnold recommends that we return to our great religious text—the Bible—and read it with a proper attention to the literary qualities of scriptural language. Our understanding of scripture must be exposed to the full range of literary experience. This is a discipline of great difficulty since it deals with words and metaphors which are 'thrown out' at objects which can be neither fully grasped nor defined: the assent thus achieved is of the whole man: it is not forced upon us but 'won', or grown into. The language of scripture can never be adequate, but it acquires a 'propriety' of its own as a result of its having been 'consecrated by use and religious feeling'. Thus our understanding of biblical language is a function of our understanding of culture.

Although this position is one which is open to attack from later biblical scholarship—as one exegete remarks, the Bible does not become beautiful until 1611—it is not naïve, since it gives due weight to the determining power of the social context, and especially of the literary culture, upon our religious beliefs.

As a theologian, Arnold states paradoxes which he is unable to resolve, but which stand for a continuing position. Poetically, this position is stated in 1855 in the *Stanzas on the Grande Chartreuse* as one of

> Wandering between two worlds, one dead,
> The other powerless to be born.

But is this an exact statement of where Arnold stands? His theological efforts in *St. Paul and Protestantism* and *Literature and Dogma*, because fuller and more explicit, enable us to see why this is not an accurate statement, but also why *The Scholar-Gipsy* and *Dover Beach* are theologically more adequate than the *Grande Chartreuse*. They are also better poetry.

The paradoxes stated by Arnold the theologian are these: we can only know, because we can only verify, clear and distinct ideas; and these include ethical ideas: 'Religion must be built on ideas about which there is no puzzle.'[25] But this is not sufficient

[25] *Last Essays on Church and Religion*, London, 1877, p. 132.

to that feeling of transcendence to which religion traditionally testifies. How do we know and express this experience of what we should now call total affirmation or commitment? Is it of 'a power not ourselves which makes for righteousness', or of 'morality touched by emotion'?

A second paradox arises from the fact that in the past this emotion has been aroused socially by ecclesiastical rites and symbols; but traditional religious institutions and language are now dead, since they are based upon a metaphysical mistake—*anthropomorphism*.

The decline in religious rites and symbols has, however, been compensated for by a rise in the interest in poetry; so it is poetry which will keep alive the mystical, the sense of affirmation, the emotion which touches morality into transcendence: 'the strongest part of our religion today is its unconscious poetry.'

But poetry depends upon a social vitality or healthy culture, so we still need an established social structure to reach down into the hearts of the people and to preserve the essential poetry of religion. The Church is still needed, so is the Christian religion; but although 'men cannot do without it', they 'cannot do with it as it is'.

To understand the paradoxes which Arnold's theology attempts to resolve helps us to appreciate more fully the nature of his success in *The Scholar-Gipsy*. Although the poem was projected in 1848, it was probably not written until May 1853; but it antedates the theological writings. Its success arises from the power of the image of the scholar gipsy to hold diverse states of mind in a successful unity.

The poem opens with a deliberately mannered evocation of a dead pastoral convention; and it is as the poet's eye travels down to Oxford's towers that the image of the gipsy emerges. Although they are both wanderers between two worlds, Arnold does not identify himself completely with the gipsy—'And I myself seem half to know thy looks'; and the world of nature which the gipsy still inhabits—'the warm, green-muffled Cumner hills'—is described in a series of careful details, which do not coalesce, as in Wordsworth, to disclose a living Nature. It is a world in which the gipsy is apostrophized as

> twirling in thy hand a wither'd spray
> And waiting for the spark from Heaven to fall.

The contrast reaches a climax at: 'But what—I dream!', and Arnold wakes from the past the gipsy inhabits to the present. The gipsy possesses a unified sensibility—'*One* aim, *one* business, *one* desire'—which is no longer possible; and in waiting for the spark from Heaven to fall, is he not therefore deluded? Thus he wanders 'like a truant *boy*' (my italics); and our curse is that we *know* that this spark from Heaven cannot fall, and we can be no more than

> light half-believers of our casual creeds.

Yet it is a question that is posed: Arnold returns to it in *Thyrsis*, written some twelve years later, when he speaks of

> A fugitive and gracious light he seeks,
> Shy to illumine; and I seek it too.

It is in *Thyrsis* also that the agent of dissociation is most clearly realized: it is the city, with its 'harsh, heart-wearying roar'. Here is the centre of that mental infection—'which though it gives no bliss yet spoils for rest'—from which Arnold bids the gipsy to flee.

The contrast between this city and Oxford persists in Arnold's prose, verse, and letters; and the extent to which his 'dreaming spires' symbolize, for Arnold, the lost organic community may be gauged from the independent testimonies of Dean Church and Lacordaire. The former speaks of Oxford as being 'as like as it could be in our modern world to a Greek *polis*, or an Italian self-centred city of the Middle Ages', standing 'by itself in its meadows by the rivers'.[26] Lacordaire's description is even more vivid: 'We have nothing like it in France. Here the university is a whole world.'[27]

The Scholar-Gipsy ends on a note of unconscious irony. Arnold was later to condemn romantic poetry for being too subjective and too unconnected with great public ideas and actions. He concludes his poem with an image—the Tyrian trader—drawn from an historical theory that the earliest inhabitants of Britain

[26] R. W. Church, *The Oxford Movement*, London, 1891, p. 139.

[27] In a letter of March 1852, Lacordaire speaks of the 'noiseless streets terminating in vistas of trees and meadows. . . . You cross silent quadrangles, meeting here and there young men wearing a curious cap and gown; no crowd, no noise; a gravity in the air as well as in the walls darkened by age, for it seems to me that nothing is repaired here for fear of committing a crime against antiquity' (*Lacordaire*, Lancelot C. Sheppard, 1964, p. 128).

were Iberians: it is an attempt to apply his principles and to generalize his reference from the subjective symbol of the gipsy to the public symbol of the trader. Yet the trader, once he is interpreted, evaporates into his interpretation; but the gipsy (like Jesus) 'lives on' with all the baffling ambiguity which provokes a further reading. The trader is a mere allegory; the gipsy succeeds in functioning symbolically. We too wander between two worlds: we can neither do without what the gipsy stands for, nor live with him as he is—'pensive and tongue-tied, in hat of antique shape, and cloak of grey'.

The achievement of *The Scholar-Gipsy* is that it is an extended metaphor of what it is to be, uniquely, modern: we seem to hold old forms of faith alongside present forms of explanation, but we remain uncertain whether we are able to associate or integrate this apparent duality: part of it seems dead, or almost inaccessible; part of it powerless to be born. The tone of lament testifies to the pain of keeping open our communications with the future, as well as with the past. It is with the *person* of the gipsy and by means of our relation to him that this duality is realized and to some extent resolved. The cognate symbol of the 'darkling plain . . . Where ignorant armies clash by night' succeeds in the same way. It derives from the same source in Thucydides as Newman's anticipation of it as a 'Night battle', where 'friend and foe stand together'.[28] What is at issue is not a clearly defined conflict between truth and error. Instead, like George Eliot, Arnold's imagination is sympathetically engaged with what he cannot accept intellectually—with Newman as with the scholar gipsy.

Arnold's poetry, where it succeeds, is acting at a deeper level than his theological notions, and therefore implies a criticism of their adequacy.[29] Where it succeeds his poetry brings divergent meanings into the explicit focus of a living symbolic unity.

His theology helps us to explicate the poem, by showing that

---

[28] *OUS*, pp. 200–1, and *Apo*, p. 428.

[29] E.g. the significance of Arnold's inclusion of the following short poem in *St. Paul and Protestantism*, p. 83:

> Below the surface-stream, shallow and light,
> Of what we *say* we feel—below the stream,
> As light, of what we *think* we feel—there flows
> With noiseless current strong, obscure and deep,
> The central stream of what we feel indeed.

it is a response to questions, theologically, and not philosophi-
cally conceived, and that it is governed by images from
Christian tradition. The scholar gipsy anticipates Renan's
Jesus (1863), whom he so much resembles, by at least ten years.

To relate the poetry to the theology helps us to avoid
Bradley's mistake of supposing the famous (or infamous) definitions to be merely clap-trap. They are attempts to keep open
our communication with the past and the future by transposing
supernatural references (*aberglaube*) into a language 'about
which there is no puzzle', or dutifully suppressing them.[30]

Arnold's limitations are less those of logic (the clarity of his
theological writings is a considerable virtue), than of feeling
(the texture of his verse is uniform and uncontested). As we
have already seen,[31] his use of metaphor lacks that density
which we find in Shakespeare or, later on, in T. S. Eliot. Even
the gipsy provokes us into inquiring what ideas he stands for: he
is almost an illustration or allegory rather than a symbol. In
Arnold's own words, his poetry is 'language *thrown out* at an
object of consciousness not fully grasped, which inspired
emotion'.[32] Used mistakenly and thus significantly of biblical
language, this expression shows by how much the language of
poetry is diminished when the poet is unable to decide whether
the experiences he refers to are of facts or subjective projections.
How are the stories about Jesus to be believed? Is Christianity a
saving fact or a saving lie?

(v) THE CATHOLIC MODERNISTS

Arnold's solution to his theological difficulties seems to anticipate that proposed by those Catholic theologians of the next
generation known as the Modernists,[33] and by George Tyrrell
in particular. Arnold came to see the future form of Christanity
as that of the Catholic Church because of what that Church has
managed to preserve of past tradition. The Church is the sole
remaining organ of conservation. Purged of its 'sacerdotal des-

[30] Renan's observation copied down by Arnold in his notebook for 1882: 'La
négation du surnatural est devenue un dogme absolu pour tout esprit cultivé'
(*Notebooks*, ed. H. F. Lowry *et al.*, Oxford, 1952, p. 378).

[31] See above, p. 25.

[32] *Literature and Dogma*, p. 30.

[33] The chief figures were, in France, Alfred Loisy (1857–1940), and in England,
George Tyrrell, S. J. (1861–1909) and Baron Friedrich von Hügel (1852–1925).

potism' and 'superannuated dogma',[34] 'its forms will be re-
tained, as symbolising with the force and charm of poetry a few
cardinal facts and ideas, simple indeed, but indispensable and
inexhaustible, and on which our race could lay hold only by
materialising them'. The 'real superiority' of the Catholic
Church 'is in its charm for the imagination—its poetry. I persist
in thinking that Catholicism has, from this superiority, a great
future before it'. Its poetry arises from 'its own age-long
growth . . . unconscious, popular, profoundly rooted, all-
enveloping'.

Like Arnold, George Tyrrell saw himself as being between
Scylla and Charybdis, that is between the two worlds of rational
explanation and traditional Christian metaphors and symbols.
These the Church had preserved like 'a fly in amber, or like a
mammoth in ice'. They were not facts or experiences but *merely*
analogues or metaphors of those experiences: 'Now there is no
valid inference from analogues; the conclusion is vitiated with
all the inexactness of the premise.' Thus the two systems of
explanation, like the two worlds they derive from, are incompatible and must be placed 'side by side like two snakes eyeing
one another': 'neither can yield to the other without suicide.'[35]
The distinction is not one of degree, it is qualitative. Between
the forms of faith—metaphor, symbol, and dogma—and the
language of belief there can be no reliable connection:[36] what
relationship there is is of 'parallels in another order of reality'.[37]
Squeeze any metaphor hard enough, and it will yield poison;
and where figurative statements cannot be reduced to literal
statements, they are 'of no use for deductive purposes'.[38] All
that remains is the direct experience of Christ in the Church he
founded[39]—a species of ecclesiastical fundamentalism, whose
consequences are the same as those of George Eliot's conserva-

[34] 'Irish Catholicism and British Liberalism' in Matthew Arnold, *Mixed Essays*,
1880, p. 118–21.

[35] M. D. Petre, *Life of George Tyrrell*, London, 1912, ii. 215ff, Letter from Tyrrell to
Wilfrid Ward, 11 Dec. 1903.

[36] Of the 'experiences (which) are the substance of revelation', Tyrrell wrote, 'the
inspired statements are but its classical and primitive symbols, and cannot (*sic*) be
treated as premisses for deduction' (*Mediaevalism*, 1908, p. 152).

[37] *Christianity at the Cross-Roads* (1909), 1963, p. 126.

[38] Unpublished essay, *Revelation as Experience*, Heythrop Journal, xii (1971), p. 140.
See also *Through Scylla and Charybdis*, 1907, p. 364.

[39] *Christianity at the Cross-Roads*, p. 178.

tism: no principles are provided by which subsequent adaptations and developments may be authenticated. Tyrrell's denial of the possibility of knowledge gained from analogy, yet his insistence that the Catholic Church alone had preserved in all its fullness 'the idea of Jesus', but only in the sense that 'no essential element had been dropped',[40] does not merely remind us of Arnold, it establishes the justice of Bremond's contemporary judgement that one-third of Tyrrell was Arnold.[41] In spite of his somewhat peremptory tone, Tyrrell was writing deliberately rather than dogmatically, and describing a dilemma from its theological side which characterized the age. When Roman Catholics expressed themselves in this fashion, however, the response of authority was negative. It repressed and persecuted. And it is possible to argue that the so-called Modernist 'movement' was created by the actions of papal authority, which not only provided the answers before the questions were asked (as Loisy remarked) but enforced them as a second Syllabus of Errors in the Decree *Lamentabili Sane Exitu* of 3 July 1907. As the French theologian Laberthonnière remarked, it seemed like a case of faith without belief being confronted by belief without faith—a confrontation which ended as an explosion within a confined space. Tyrrell was excommunicated for writing in *The Times* what he had been permitted to say in his books, and von Hügel was nearly excommunicated for attending his friend's funeral.

Tyrrell's theology came to assume that 'whereas formerly men had always felt that in religion . . . truth in its most perfect form lay in the past, they were now led to think that the more perfect, and ever more perfectible, form lay in the future'.[42] This assumption—that the future would prove more knowable than the past—arose from their despair of analogy, a despair which is also to be seen in Tyrrell's highly questionable analogy that 'a moral system ought to survive its speculative roots, much as a tree retains life after it is felled'.[43]

Theologians as much as novelists seemed to face the same question: how are the stories about Jesus to be believed? What

---

[40] Tyrrell ('Hilaire Bourdon'), *The Church and the Future*, 1903, p. 91.

[41] Cited in A. R. Vidler, *The Modernist Movement in the Roman Church*, Cambridge, 1934, p. 159.

[42] Baron Friedrich von Hügel, *Selected Letters*, ed. Bernard Holland, repr. 1928, p. 15.

[43] *George Tyrrell's Letters*, ed. M. D. Petre, London, 1920, p. 68.

is the reality to which they refer? The answers given by Arnold and Tyrrell have a common factor which I have defined as Modernist. Nowhere is this quality more exactly defined than it is by the contemporary philosopher, R. B. Braithwaite. He defines a religious belief as 'the assertion of an intention to carry out a certain behaviour policy, subsumable under a sufficiently general principle to be a moral one, together with the implicit or explicit statement, but *not the assertion*, of certain stories'.[44] Braithwaite, following Arnold, specifically denies that it is necessary for the religious asserter 'to believe in the truth of the story involved in the assertions: what is necessary is that the story should be *entertained* in thought'.[45]

But if, as we have seen, great plays and novels require us to do more than merely *entertain* the stories they tell, Scripture positively obliges us to observe Coleridge's distinction between language used in aid of conviction, and language as a means of illustration. Arnold himself was aware of the danger of discarding positive names like 'God' for negative terms like 'the unknowable'. Such a position is as open now as it was then to Maurice Blondel's criticism of the Modernists—that they judged Revelation by what is unrevealed. It is 'to put the unknowable unconscious in place of the Heavenly Father'.[46]

(VI) THOMAS HARDY

The radical changing of the questions is a gradual process: without the revolutionary effects of the two world wars it might still be at issue. After George Eliot and Arnold comes Thomas Hardy, whose vision is not of fictions to be 'entertained', but of the tragic disparity between what is and what *ought* to be the case. We are confronted by this contradiction in all its force in the powerful opening to *Jude the Obscure*, where the boy Jude obeys the parting injunction of the village schoolmaster to be kind to birds, by allowing rooks to feed off the fields he is paid to guard. He is thrashed by the farmer for his pains and discovers 'the flaw in the terrestrial scheme, by which what was good for

[44] R. B. Braithwaite, *An Empiricist's View of the Nature of Religious Belief*, Cambridge, 1955 (my italics), p. 32.

[45] R. B. Braithwaite, *An Empiricist's View* . . ., p. 26 (my italics).

[46] Maurice Blondel, *History and Dogma*, trans. A. Dru and Illtyd Trethowan, London, 1964, p. 260.

God's birds was bad for God's gardener'. He goes off and lays down upon his back in a field and gazes into the sky:

The fog had by this time become more translucent, and the position of the sun could be seen through it. He pulled his straw hat over his face and peered through the interstices of the plaiting at the white brightness, vaguely reflecting. Growing up brought responsibilities, he found. Events did not rhyme quite as he had thought. Nature's logic was too horrid for him to care for. That mercy towards one set of creatures was cruelty towards another sickened his sense of harmony.[47]

Hardy's imagination diffuses and dissipates the world of Jude's expectations—'the heavenly Jerusalem' of Christ-minster—into the horrifying world of Father Time, who was 'Age masquerading as Juvenility', a boy 'of a sort unknown in the last generation—the outcome of new views of life. They seem to see all its terrors before they are old enough to have staying power to resist them.'[48] Yet Hardy's vision of the conflict between belief and unbelief seems little different from that of the Catholic Modernists: 'At present intellect in Christ-minster is pushing one way, and religion the other; and so they stand stock-still, like two rams butting each other.'[49] This irresolvable tension is at the heart of the relation between Jude and Sue who seem 'to be one person split in two';[50] but it is to the experience of ancient Rome, rather than to an enlightened future, that Hardy looks for his explanation:

Thy aëriel part, and all the fiery parts which are mingled in thee, though by nature they have an upward tendency, still in obedience to the disposition of the universe they are overpowered here in the compound mass the body.[51]

Is Feuerbach's prophecy once again fulfilled? As the tragedy moves to its climax, and we suffer the 'realization' of the predicates—'love, wisdom, and justice'—so we are led to a changed understanding of their subject—'Providence'—as, perhaps, no more than the 'unweeting spinner of the years'. Yet, like George Eliot, Hardy's transvaluation is not total. The traditional metaphors of religious description are retained as

[47] *Jude the Obscure*, London, 1923, p. 15.
[48] *Jude The Obscure*, pp. 346, 424.
[49] Ibid, p. 186.
[50] Ibid, p. 287.
[51] Ibid, p. 320.

essential mediating structures: they are not *mere* similes. When, at a turning-point in the narrative, Jude burns his theological books, Hardy distinguishes what Jude continues to *believe*, from what he is no longer obliged to profess;[52] and he dies with Job's questions on his lips:[53]

> 'Wherefore is light given to him that is in misery,
> and life unto the bitter in soul?'

What has changed is the ease or certainty with which we can interpret these analogues which still direct our experience:

The meditative world is older, more invidious, more nervous, more quizzical, than it once was, and being unhappily perplexed by—
> Riddles of Death Thebes never knew,

may be less ready and less able than Hellas and old England were to look through the insistent, and often grotesque, substance at the thing signified.[54]

Yet, the quality in Hardy that D. H. Lawrence felt to be the source of his weakness—that what brings destruction is the lesser transgression against the social code, rather than that against a greater, uncomprehended morality or fate—is what anchors his vision within the substance of a society. Hardy is still within a tradition that embraces Wordsworth and Coleridge: poetry and religion still 'touch each other, or rather modulate into each other'.[55] But the changing questions may be felt behind the breakdown of the grammar—a fact which is most sharply registered in changing attitudes to Nature. For Wordsworth, Nature spoke rememberable things. For Arnold, however, the descriptive details do not coalesce to disclose a living voice (a position the full consequences of which Mill does not anticipate when he testifies to the power of Wordsworth's poetry in overcoming 'a crisis in my mental history'). But if, for Arnold, God is not dead, but hidden, for Hardy his presence is further diminished to that of fellow sufferer who, 'in conscious-ness of life's tears', has made us a humble pioneer of himself—'we have reached feeling faster than he' (*A Fragment*). In the *Woodlanders* the mood is that of the Lesser Celandine general-

---

[52] *Jude the Obscure*, p. 273. 'He might go on believing as before, but he professed nothing, and no longer owned and exhibited engines of faith which, as their proprietor, he might naturally be supposed to exercise on himself first of all.'

[53] Ibid., p. 510.

[54] Preface to *The Dynasts*, London, 1903, p. xi.

[55] Apology, *Late Lyrics and Earlier* (1922).

ized—the stars disclose 'no detailed design' but, like the lanterns of the Woodlanders, they are 'eyes weary with watching'.

The flat-footed nature of Hardy's references to the 'President of the Immortals' and the 'unweeting spinner of the years' arises not from unbelief but from a kind of theological malnutrition, for which he is not responsible. Instead his position is one, not so much of agnosticism, as of carefully circumscribed theological *continence*. He was, as he says, 'not a theorist'; and what he held was often beyond his power to explain in the theological terms then available. Hence his sympathy with the Modernists, whom he calls the New Catholics who, in 'making a struggle for continuity by applying the principle of evolution to their own faith', might have succeeded in 'outflanking the hesitating English instinct towards liturgical restatement'—'a flank march which I at the time quite expected to witness, with the gathering of many millions of waiting agnostics into its fold'. Instead the New Catholics had been thrown over by 'the once august hierarchy of Rome' who had, thereby, 'lost its chance of being the religion of the future'.[56]

However short-winded or home-made Hardy's attempts at explicitness may seem to be, therefore, they are always well-informed. The achievement of such final lines as 'hoping it might be so' (*The Oxen*), or 'thus I; faltering forward' (*The Voice*), or the suggestion of a 'new bell's boom' in *Afterwards* is that of an exactitude of poetic statement which is also an exactitude of theological statement. What is defined is an unresolved and continuing crisis of belief. A present lack of vision is seen simply in terms of loss, not of a perverted consciousness needing to be reduced to clear essentials. In later life, Wordsworth sees by glimpses, and, as age comes on, may scarcely see at all. Coleridge sees, not feels, how beautiful things are. Even later, for Hopkins, although God's glory may no longer be made manifest sacramentally in the stars, still the finger of God finds him: the problem is how to share the present with the past; how to move through the essentially different metaphors of the present to 'the thing signified'.

---

[56] In Apology (Feb. 1922) to *Late Lyrics and Earlier*. In 1925 Hardy told Frédéric Lefèvre that 'the religion which ought to be preserved if the world is not to perish' was 'an alliance of rationalism and religion (which) would be created by poetry'.

4

T. S. Eliot's Grammar of Poetry and Belief

I. Four Quartets

(1) THE 'PARATACTIC' FORM OF FAITH

In *Four Quartets* Eliot achieves the difficult resolution. By means of, and not in spite of his poetry, he shows how we may still be certain of what is obscurely revealed. As early as 1927, in a note which significantly he did not republish,[1] he had asserted that 'doubt and uncertainty are merely a variety of belief'. He goes on to say that although those like Arnold who wander 'between two worlds' are 'living parasitically . . . on the minds of the men of genius of the past who have believed something', yet this 'is better than not living at all'.

The position which Eliot confronts is exemplified in its extreme form by James Joyce in *A Portrait of the Artist*. Its hero, Stephen Dedalus, ends where he began, 'supersaturated with the religion in which you say you disbelieve'. Neither believing, nor disbelieving, in 'the vesture of a doubting monk',[2] who quotes Augustine and Newman at the threshold of 'liberation', Stephen denies that he is going 'to become a protestant': 'What kind of liberation would that be,' he asks, 'to forsake an absurdity which is logical and coherent and to embrace one which is illogical and incoherent?'[3] Like Arnold before him, he cannot live with 'the faith', but can he live without it?

Joyce's intention is to show how Stephen, like the legendary Daedalus, whose name he bears, the cunning artificer, successfully flies from his enemies. But the references to classical mythology conceal the failure to realize this liberation. When Stephen 'seems to see the winged form flying above the waves and slowly climbing the air', he interprets it as symbolizing prophetically the liberated Daedalus. The reader, however, is more justly reminded of his less successful son, Icarus, since at

---

[1] 'A Note on Poetry and Belief', in *The Enemy*, Jan. 1927, pp. 15–17.
[2] James Joyce, *A Portrait of the Artist as a Young Man* (1916), Penguin edn., 1964, pp. 176, 239, 240.
[3] James Joyce, *A Portrait of the Artist as a Young Man*, p. 243.

the end Stephen is still confronting a religion he can neither do without, nor do with as it is. Is this state of oscillation a state of paralysis, or is all oscillation between two worlds a form of faith?

Such a condition, in which extremes invoke their opposites may be, as T. S. Eliot remarks, 'either a vision or a nightmare': 'The human mind is perpetually driven between two desires . . . each of which may be either a vision or a nightmare: the vision and nightmare of the material world, and the vision and night-mare of the immaterial. . . . We move, *outside of the Christian faith*, between the terror of the purely irrational and the horror of the purely rational.'[4]

Stephen's contradictions remain unresolved. They are be-tween a rationality which is 'absurd', and the flesh from which he recoils as 'profane'. Are these visions which elude him, or nightmares that threaten? Is he within or outside faith?

Eliot's answer is a radical one. To have faith it is not neces-sary to believe 'the same things in the same way'. For him, as for Newman, religious belief has been, historically and necessarily, 'in constant mutation'. It is for this reason that doubt and uncertainty are a variety of belief: they are the agents of its development. It is therefore Eliot's hope that: 'Christianity will probably continue to modify itself, as in the past, into some-thing that can be believed in.'

This raises the general question: for well over a century we have spoken of ourselves as being on the way or in transition from past illusions to new and liberated forms of consciousness. Inherited beliefs have been conceived as but the means, ac-cidentally, by which the process is triggered off; and it is the ethical predicates (love, truth, and justice) or the liberated imagination which are the realities: these are the nouns, for which, for example, 'God' is but the adjective or qualifier. To feel the proper force of these assertions is for the believer to ask whether he does not inevitably have to experience his religion as a 'projection', in which for example, 'great feelings will often take the aspect of error, and great faith the aspect of illusion?'[5] From this, it is but a step to Ibsen's 'take the saving lie from the average man and you take his happiness away, too . . . because

[4] In *Revelation*, ed. John Baillie and Hugh Martin, London, 1937, pp. 31–2, 36 (my italics).
[5] George Eliot, *Middlemarch*, Oxford, 1950, p. 896.

that lie is the stimulating principle of life.'⁶ What is chiefly significant is that, for us, as for the writers so far discussed, these questions remain obstinately open still. Can we speak of a unique change of consciousness if it is unable to develop beyond its *locus classicus*—its first statements in Feuerbach and Arnold? Those of us who continue to wait for God rather than Godot, continue also to practise the secret discipline of reading the Greek philosophers, St. Augustine, St. Anselm, Shakespeare, Newman—and the Gospels, as if we could still understand them, and they could still 'find' us. Was Coleridge right in calling 'adherence to the past and ancient, the desire and the admiration of permanence', *religious*? What, then, is the uniqueness we experience? We certainly observe an accelerated rate of change, and this in turn appears to deny any point of rest or stability within the process. Thus, if we seek for what is ever ancient, ever new, we may recognize what is ancient, and what is new, but not their connection: the rate of acceleration creates a social structure in which such stereoscopic focusing becomes uniquely implausible.

What, I would suggest, is unique to the later nineteenth century (and still largely to ours) is the expectation that somehow the paradoxes I have been describing ought to be clarified and *reduced* to a single or univocal meaning. Arnold's image of the tranquil, enfolding sea of faith in *Dover Beach* is more applicable to the decline of religious vitality in the late Middle Ages than to its creative ferment in the thirteenth century. What we have unconsciously absorbed from nineteenth-century writers may be an expectation of greater peace and stability than we are entitled to have—politically and religiously—if we wish to stay alive and grow towards the light; there may be words and myths which are simply uninvertible; and it may be fruitless to seek to *reduce* them to other forms of explanation which, although rationally more satisfactory, are inadequate to the character of the experiences themselves.

What we have learned since Arnold is how more exactly to conceive our choice. To ask if a religion is true is not to make choices between false nouns and true adjectives, or between anthropomorphisms and the ideas they stand for. It is to conceive the choice as one between a *reduction* to a single focus, and

⁶ Henrik Ibsen, *The Wild Duck* (1884), Act V.

an affirmation which requires for its condition a double or stereoscopic focusing. What makes the latter an act of *religious* imagination is when we describe the polarity we experience as being between the present—the sceptical world of everyday sense, which Arnold calls that of 'facts', which can be empirically verified—and the past—the believing world, and in particular that of those religious events and values which cannot thus be verified. The believer accepts polarity, not to rest in a contradiction, but because he believes that the two worlds are neither dead nor unborn, but mutually alive; and within the form of this apparent paradox, this tension within unity, by saying and unsaying, he lives out the *development* of those beliefs he has inherited.

Arnold was right. Whether our beliefs are true or false is a question which has to be located (if it is to be resolved) within that activity we call 'imagination'. This is the warning which Arnold, the poet, hands to Arnold, the theologian. What he overlooked in theory (but not always in practice) was the inescapably contested nature of that activity. Its polar or 'paratactic'[7] form is, in fact, a traditional characteristic of religious expression. This is why we require for our conception of Christianity, for example, something more complex than the image of a single unifying focus—a circle with one centre. As von Hügel noted, it may be truer to conceive religion as an ellipse with two foci[8]—other-worldlines, this-worldliness; or the past and the present. For Coleridge, polarity is the constitutive characteristic of imagination: 'the polar forces are the two forms, in which one power works in the same act and instant.' In the *Biographia Literaria*,[9] he writes of 'this power, first put in action by the will

---

[7] That is, by juxtaposition rather than logical sequence—a phenomenon noted by J. Huizinga in *The Waning of the Middle Ages* (1924), and interpreted by Erich Auerbach in *Mimesis* (1946) as characterizing medieval Christian sensibility. The habit of so juxtaposing, for example, Old Testament and New Testament images and themes (Adam and Christ), or characters and events as, for example, in the *Chanson de Roland*, transforms them into 'figures—as on the sarcophagi of late antiquity—(which) are placed side by side paratactically. They no longer have any reality, they have only signification' (*Mimesis*, repr. 1971, p. 116). See also Rosamond Tuve on 'Herbert's method' of producing new meanings, by similarly juxtaposing images from the Old and New Testaments in *A Reading of George Herbert*, 1932, esp. pp. 61–3.

[8] This image, suggested by Ernest Troeltsch (1865–1923), is discussed by von Hügel in *Eternal Life*, London, 1912, pp. 199–200.

[9] *BL*, chap. xv, p. 151.

and understanding, . . . (which) reveals itself in the balance or reconcilement of opposite or discordant qualities.'

One hundred and fifty years after Coleridge, Yevtuschenko speaks of himself as 'like a train/rushing for many years now/between the city of Yes/and the city of No.' The soviet poet refuses to escape by invoking the metaphor of 'transition'. Instead he affirms that he lives only as he lets his 'nerves be strained' between such polarities as those which Arnold and Joyce, for example, attempt to reduce. Yet, as I have suggested, the transition from the superseded world to one epiphanized and emancipated no more takes place for Stephen Dedalus than it does for the author of *The Scholar-Gipsy*: both remain between two worlds. My argument has been that wherever poets and novelists conceive their experience in such terms, this may be a sign of the persistence of religious imagination.

This is certainly a characteristic of the religious awareness of writers as various as Dostoevsky and the war poet Wilfred Owen. Under the stress of battle, Owen experienced in himself the dissociative dualism realized by Dostoevsky in such characters as Ivan and Dmitri Karamazov, Stavrogin, and Raskolnikov (whose very name suggests a split, or '*raskolot*'). They oscillate, often violently, between belief and unbelief, good and evil. In Owen's case, his sufferings did not cause him to abandon religion, but he could only accept it in an agonizingly contested form which he expresses in images of sharp discontinuity—'what passing-bells for these who die as cattle?'[10] Thus he speaks of 'a point where prayer is indistinguishable from blasphemy',[11] and of himself as a 'Primitive Christian',[12] who is becoming 'more and more Christian as I walk the unchristian ways of Christendom'.[13]

To rest content in such a state of oscillation can be, at its worst, dissociative or 'alienating'; at its mildest it is 'parasitic'. Dostoevsky was driven to conclude that these tendencies could be resolved only within the Christian faith. By recourse to the

---

[10] *The Collected Poems of Wilfred Owen*, ed. C. Day Lewis, 1963, p. 44.
[11] Jon Stallworthy, *Wilfred Owen*, OUP, 1977, p. 258.
[12] Stallworthy, *Wilfred Owen*, p. 187.
[13] Ibid., p. 185.

unifying image of Christ, and by giving 'yourself wholly up to Him, the pain of your duality will be thereby alleviated'.[14]

In *Four Quartets* Eliot shows how that alleviation can be gained without the sacrifice of imaginative integrity, since although imagination must first dissolve, diffuse, and dissipate, in order to re-create, it does not follow that a language which the poetic imagination has thus dislocated must remain a heap of broken images. We ought to expect it to be re-created in that greater rational and discursive adequacy we may properly call belief. This is what it is for the imaginative act to be completed, when the new signs become anchored in the thing signified.

(II) 'SAYING AND UNSAYING TO A POSITIVE RESULT'

It is Eliot's achievement in *Four Quartets* to show how much a poet can affirm without compromising the integrity of his imagination. In religion, as Eliot shows, an appeal to imagination goes farther than merely diffusing or dissipating a prior doubt: it affirms—a fact which every common reader knows, but one which many critics and philosphers deny. Eliot establishes how 'doubt and uncertainty are a variety of belief' by showing how 'years of living among the breakage/Of what was believed in as the most reliable' makes it possible, in the end, to pray 'the unprayable prayer'.[15]

To begin with, let us consider the objections. They are the following. Although overlaps between religion and imagination have occurred, this is a historical accident merely; and our practice today is correct—to affirm not the relationship, but the distinction. Furthermore, to speak of grounding religious assent in those forms—metaphor and symbol—which are peculiarly imaginative seems to be flying in the face of religious history, since to contend that religious belief must be credible to imagination is to overlook the obvious claim that it must first be reasonable. Has not religious belief always been incompatible with the free play of imagination? The aim of literature is to please, that of religion to press questions of truth. And even if a case could be made out in theory, directly we turn to religious

---

[14] *Letters of F. M. Dostoevsky to his family and friends*, ed. Mayne, E. T., 1962, p. 249. In an earlier letter (p. 71) Dostoevsky answers Shatov's question in *The Devils* affirmatively: 'But didn't you tell me that if it were mathematically proved to you that truth was outside Christ, you would rather remain with Christ than with truth?' (E. T., Penguin edn., p. 255).

[15] *DS* II (see above, pp. 124f.).

poetry we shall see how religious belief inhibits imaginative power. Literary critics assume that it is a weakness for poetry to be explicitly religious, and religious poetry is accordingly regarded as a species of minor or attenuated poetry.

The best way to reply to such objections is to show, by the close reading of a text, how a grammar begins to emerge when, for example, a theologian responds to questions raised by a literary critic. In discussing *Four Quartets*, for example, the literary critic may ask whether, as the religious significance of the poem grows more explicit, so the poetry weakens. This question is implied in Dr F. R. Leavis's later judgements of *Four Quartets*, when he writes: 'I have emphasized Eliot's continence of affirmation. But as we go through the subsequent quartets we find the specifically Christian note becoming stronger.'[16] It may also be detected in an earlier warning—that, when the theologian attempts to elucidate a poem, he tends to frustrate the poet's labours, which are to circumvent 'at every level what may be called *cliché*'.[17] Dr Johnson makes a similar assumption.[18] 'The ideas of Christian theology are too simple for eloquence, too sacred for fiction.' Religion does not require to be recommended by poetry, or its theological ideas to be diffused or dissipated by imagination. Such as it is, religious truth is known already. It is a fair inference to add the further argument that, in writing religious poetry, the poet is under an obligation to say what he *ought* to feel, not what he fully feels. Thus, the poet who writes of his religious belief will be under a similar restriction to the critic. His feelings will be restricted by a sense of obligation; and he will tend to deal not in images fresh with the dew upon them, but in clichés—and in theological clichés at that. He will have arrived, without having travelled. Let us take as an example Newman's poem *The Pillar of the Cloud* which, significantly, one remembers as a hymn, *Lead, Kindly Light*. I choose it because I find its sentiments devotionally useful 'I do not ask to see/The distant scene—one step enough for me.' This, by any standards, is memorable speech, but directly I reach the lines:

[16] *English Literature in our time and the University*, London, 1969, pp. 130, 154.
[17] *Scrutiny*, xv. 64, repub. in *The Common Pursuit*, 1952, p. 287.
[18] *Life of Waller*, in *Lives of the Poets*, Oxford, 1906, i. 211–12.

> So long Thy power hath blest me, sure it still
>   Will lead me on,
> O'er moor and fen, o'er crag and torrent, till
>   The night is gone;
> And with the morn those angel faces smile
> Which I have loved long since, and lost awhile.

I, too, wake up: the pressure, such as it was, behind the opening words has gone: these are spiritual clichés.

Is this not what also happens in a subtler and longer form in *Four Quartets* in the transition from *Burnt Norton* to *Little Gidding*? After all, we have been warned. Has not the author himself claimed that 'literary criticism should be completed by criticism from a definite ethical and theological standpoint'?[19] May we not expect, therefore, that we shall move from the poetically effective questionings of *Burnt Norton* to the 'answers' in *Little Gidding*, which, since they are of a theological nature, will be clichés precisely because they are theologically conceived? Thus, in proportion as the poem becomes religiously more explicit, so its force as poetry is bound to become weaker.

The first thing a theologian notices is that the explicitness, such as it is, is interwoven with as much, if not more, scepticism and despair as is expressed by the writers already considered. What is different is the momentum and tone. By comparison with Eliot, Arnold's despair is positively buoyant, and Hardy's scepticism short-winded. The momentum of *Four Quartets* is such as to invite one to read it as if its structure were circular, or more exactly, a spiral. In order to understand, we must read round and round. And what further encourages this form of reading—in a descending spiral—is the poet's tone. It recalls that earlier invitation in *Prufrock*:

> Let us go then, you and I,
> When the evening is spread out against the sky,

and part of the effect of the momentum of *Four Quartets* is to encourage us to keep up this conversation. Thus Eliot avoids the slightest suggestion of talking *at* us, in the manner of Arnold, or of Yeats, who declaims that: 'The best lack all conviction, while the worst/are full of passionate intensity.'

There is a second observation of a theological kind which

[19] T. S. Eliot, 'Religion and Literature', in *Selected Essays*, 3rd edn., London, 1969, p. 388.

arises from the question posed by the literary critic. Is the religious 'explicitness' of the poem where one expects it to be—namely, at the 'end', that is in the last quartet, *Little Gidding*?

It might be just as easy to claim that it is the first movement, *Burnt Norton*, which is the most explicit. It has been commended for its creation of concepts; and this it does in language reminiscent of F. H. Bradley in *Appearance and Reality*, where he says, for example, 'the emotion we attend to is, taken strictly, never precisely the same thing as the emotion which we feel'.[20] By coming so close to the language of philosophical explanation, Eliot could be said (in this movement) to be especially concerned to *generalize* his meaning.

A further factor is that in each of the quartets there is a movement (Part V) dealing with the intolerable wrestle with meaning. It is in this recurring section that the poet's agony seems to be most directly and explicitly realized; and any attempt towards a more explicitly religious statement is always preceded by such a movement, which is related to it. Thus, it is only after speaking of words straining and decaying with imprecision that we are told 'the Word in the desert is most attacked by voices of temptation'.[21]

The preceding talk about language seems to be offered as a guide to *how* we are to understand the subseqent talk about the Word of God. Similarly, in movement II of *East Coker*, the final statement that 'humility is endless' is preceded by a thorough description of *how* we become humble in terms of our unsuccessful attempts to express ourselves in a 'worn-out poetical fashion', and in our equally unsuccessful attempt to derive knowledge from experience. This prepares us for what, on first reading, is the enigmatic statement in Movement V that, 'Old men ought to be explorers.' But, if we are reading the poem for the second time round, then it is as we remember the next quartet, *The Dry Salvages*, that this remark will be clarified.

What I want to suggest is that it is in this, the penultimate quartet, rather than in the last, *Little Gidding*, that the most explicitly theological and religious references seem to be concentrated. Yet it is also where the poetry is most substantially

---

[20] *Appearance and Reality*, 1893, p. 521.
[21] *BN* V.

personal and autobiographical in its reference, and where the imagery of Eastern Point, off which lie the rocks known as the Dry Salvages, is most topographically precise. I want especially to concentrate on movement II, to suggest that in this movement Eliot is doing more than showing 'continence' in his handling of religious meanings and in making them explicit. This very explicitness is preceded by and seems dependent upon a prior dissolution and negation, not merely of crude religious clichés, but of customary, even orthodox, modes of conception. For example, 'the Prayer of the one Annunciation' is qualified as 'being hardly, barely prayable'; and how this is so is established in the stanzas preceding. It is like being in 'a drifting boat with a slow leakage', or bringing in 'a haul that will not bear examination'. Similarly, the conclusion in movement V that in Incarnation the past and future are 'conquered and reconciled' is certainly not stated thus crudely. Once more it is in terms of 'the unattended Moment, the moment in and out of time./The distraction fit, lost in a shaft of sunlight'; and it is further qualified by being spoken of as 'only hints and guesses', and as a gift therefore 'only half understood'. But it is in what is almost the firmest and most substantial passage in the whole poem—that on the dry salvages, the rocks themselves—that all the meanings, biographical, topographical and religious, are brought most sharply into focus:

> And the ragged rock in the restless waters,
> Waves wash over it, fogs conceal it;
> On a halcyon day it is merely a monument,
> In navigable weather it is always a seamark
> To lay a course by: but in the sombre season
> Or the sudden fury, is what it always was. (*DS* II)

Sensing an ambiguity in the poet's reference to 'salvages', one asks whether this description does not imply that as we are destroyed ('savaged'), so we are saved; or, in the words of *East Coker* (IV, st. 2), 'that, to be restored, our sickness must grow worse'. But it is this movement (IV) of *East Coker* which states explicitly what may be implied in the later quartet, *The Dry Salvages* (and not the other way round). However, it is the passages on either side of this description of the 'dry salvages' which interest me most as a theologian. I refer to:

It seems, as one becomes older,
That the past has another pattern, and ceases to be a
　　mere sequence—
Or even development: the latter a partial fallacy
Encouraged by superficial notions of evolution,
Which becomes, in the popular mind, a means of
　　disowning the past.　　　　　　　(*DS* II, st. 7)

I sometimes wonder if that is what Krishna meant—
Among other things—or one way of putting the same thing:
That the future is a faded song, a Royal Rose or a
　　lavender spray
Of wistful regret for those who are not yet here to
　　regret,
Pressed between yellow leaves of a book that has never
　　been opened.　　　　　　　　(*DS* III, st. 1)

It is important to bear in mind Eliot's conception of tradition, and of received or customary conceptions of how we come to believe in Christian doctrine, and in what sense that belief has developed. The problem of how there is continuity with the past is sometimes solved optimistically by conceiving this development as a chain of inferences, which can be systematically demonstrated, even 'numbered'. The Modernists, less optimistically, used an evolutionary model, and true developments of doctrine were those which had shown themselves fittest to survive, so that Alfred Loisy could assert that the Church had to become what is has become, or, more ironically, 'Jésus annonçait le royaume et c'est l'église qui est venue.'[22] In his prose writing, Eliot's conception of tradition is very close to Newman's (or Coleridge's) understanding of doctrinal development. But there is a subtle reservation which it is easy to overlook. When he speaks of the existing monuments of a culture as forming an ideal order, and of that order as being ever so slightly altered, by the introduction of the really new work of art, his conclusion is that the past is 'altered by the present as much as the present is directed by the past'.[23]

To turn to the passages from *The Dry Salvages* I have cited is to see this reservation as becoming central. Development (not just the cliché, but even the customary sense?) seems to be dis-

[22] *The Gospel and the Church*, iv. 3. (E.T., 1903, pp. 150, 166.)
[23] *SE*, p. 15.

missed as a 'partial fallacy'. What we, the old men, grow into unwillingly, is what they, the young men, will remember nostalgically: our future is their 'faded song': the most we achieve is somebody else's past. The development of belief, far from being a simple *transition*, to be sought after and relished, may be what our shortcomings oblige us to suffer.

It is significant that Eliot, like Newman, does not press the distinction between the primary forms of religious faith and the language of the beliefs and doctrines derived from them. In his use of such key words as 'annunciation', 'prayer', and 'time', he proceeds by 'rejection and elimination'[24] to say and unsay to a positive result. Thus his way of being religiously explicit, far from relapsing into cliché, seems deliberately to deny any such easy consolation, and to put the onus of interpretation upon us, the reader. 'Time is no healer', he concludes.[25] But how are we to speak these lines? Sadly or triumphantly? The tone seems left to us to supply, as if the poet wishes to keep such statements open to various answers, and to keep them from closing up into a dogmatic, definitive, or univocal *answer*. It is for the reader in the end to achieve his own form of the difficult resolution. Although this is subtler than his use, in *The Waste Land*, of the refrain 'Shantih, Shantih, Shantih', the intention is the same: how he speaks the words is for the reader to decide. In *The Waste Land* a clue is given in the notes; but is the refrain merely the disguise for, or equivalent of, the all too familiar cliché—'The peace which passeth understanding'? As Christopher Ricks has pointed out, mixed tones contend; they also, by contending, keep the *form* of the affirmations as closely as possible to the form of the initial questions.[26]

In *Four Quartets*, Eliot's explicit religious statement seems thus to depend upon a prior negation and diffusion of clichés, even 'orthodox' conceptions, so that, where the religious significance is most explicit, it is often most contested, as well as being farthest from cliché. And what seems to be bound up with this,

[24] *SE*, p. 408.
[25] *DS* III, st. 1.
[26] This is a method similar to that employed by the authors of the gospels, particularly John, cp. Newman on the text of Scripture: 'The bearing and drift of the narrative are not given.' Instead, they may be variously interpreted 'according to the accidental tone of mind in the reader'. 'Holy Scripture in its relation to the Catholic Creed' (1838), in *Discussions and Arguments*, London, 1872, pp. 174–8.

as being the means by which the intention can be accepted as having been convincingly evoked, is the recurring effort to achieve (by discussing it) linguistic integrity. Wordsworth also makes similar efforts for similar reasons in the *Prelude*:[27] each poet speaks of his difficulty in evoking 'unknown modes of being' as he succeeds in doing so.

In the last quartet, *Little Gidding*, however, I admit to a difficulty. The justly celebrated passage on prayer[28] begins, as we should expect, by saying what prayer is not; and the expected resolution is expressed in movement V as a resolution of verbal difficulties, where the right words are at last in the right order, with 'the complete consort dancing together'.

The poet's conclusion—that what we seek is a 'condition of complete simplicity'—is qualified (as we should expect) as 'costing not less than everything'. As I have suggested, the poet intends, not a direct description of simplicity, but an indirect one of how much it costs.

Even so, I admit to a critical difficulty with such key passages as this in movement III from Julian of Norwich:

> Sin is Behovely, but
> All shall be well, and
> All manner of things shall be well.

Is there enough pressure behind such phrases? By resorting to them, has the poetry begun to weaken? It is possible to reply that Eliot (like Milton before him) is aware of their unsatisfactoriness but that they are the only means of expressing what is already fading from our experience. As the traditional images and symbols of religion become esoteric so does the feeling which alone can give their use an adequate expressive force: 'when religious feeling disappears, the words in which men have struggled to express it become meaningless.'[29]

Once more, we are come to the edge of plausibility, when what ceases to be imaginatively plausible remains credible only to the theologian. And yet is it true that only by using such words can we identify the experiences for which they were once socially plausible explanations? Preserved 'like flies in amber',

[27] In Book v, ll. 595–605; Book vi, ll. 592–602.
[28] *LG* I, st. 3.
[29] *OPP*, p. 25.

they are analogues whose truth, if it can be realized, is not as it is flatly stated, but as it is qualified in the manner of *The Dry Salvages*. Here such terms as Annunciation, Incarnation, and the meaning and patterning of the past are given a charge which is as poetically as it is theologically effective. What their use in *Little Gidding* seems to do is to urge the reader on (or back) to the generalizing and explaining language of *Burnt Norton*, to such statements as in movement II:

> I can only say, *there* we have been: but I cannot say where.

Here is surely a Wordsworthian echo, and in particular of that statement in the *Prelude*:[30]

> but that the soul,
> Remembering how she felt, but what she felt
> Remembering not, retains an obscure sense
> Of possible sublimity.

In somewhat similar manner, both Eliot and Wordsworth are concerned to isolate in order to evoke and identify those formative 'spots of time', or what Eliot calls in a first draft of *Little Gidding* II, 'the essential moments'.[31] Neither tells us 'what' they stand for directly, but only 'how' they occur; but the 'how', when it is successfully evoked, tells us 'what'. The poetic form seems necessary, therefore, for its realization: these words have to be in these positions: the best words have to be in the best order.

This returns me to the question: *does religious explicitness weaken poetry*? If the subject-matter of religious poetry is accepted as necessarily and already defined theologically, the answer must be yes, since the range of feeling and imagination is by definition already delimited to ornamenting theological truths by declamatory odes or hymns. This was Dr Johnson's position. If a contemporary literary critic follows suit, then he is making a *theological* mistake. This is not Eliot's practice, either as poet or theologian. Now this may seem at odds with his distinction (in the essay I have already cited) between 'what we like' and 'what we *ought* to like'.[32] But this is to overlook the small print, since

---

[30] *Prelude*, ii. 315f.
[31] Helen Gardner, *The Composition of Four Quartets*, London, 1978, pp. 183, 185.
[32] *SE*, p. 399.

Eliot goes on to say that 'few people are honest enough to know either. The first means knowing what we feel: very few know that. The second involves understanding our shortcomings.' Shortcomings can be interpreted in a purely ethical or spiritual sense; but, if my reading of the *Quartets* is accurate, then it can also be interpreted as a warning against an over-confident religious explicitness of belief. In some ways the small print of Eliot's prose becomes the large print of his poetry. When, for example, a theologian reads in *Little Gidding* that

> the words sufficed
> To compel the recognition they preceded.

he may be led to ask whether, in a more general sense, Eliot's conception of Revelation is not that of 'a doctrine lying hid in language', or of what 'is awarded to us in the address that encounters us'.[33] To understand our shortcomings is certainly to submit to being made by religion; but it is also to submit to begining deep within 'projections' (in the Feuerbachian sense as understood by George Eliot), which have to be lived *with* to be lived *through*. It is to face

> Years of living among the breakage
> Of what was believed in as the most reliable—
> And therefore the fittest for renunciation[34]

This way of fashioning a meaning by opposite strokes is to be distinguished from oscillating between incompatible positions (as in Joyce's *Portrait*). It is, in Newman's words,[35] a saying and unsaying to a positive result, which is thus defined by the familiar compound ghost of *Little Gidding* (II):

> But, as the passage now presents no hindrance
> To the spirit unappeased and peregrine
> Between two worlds become much like each other,
> So I find words I never thought to speak

Eliot's reconciling use of the imagery of being between two worlds and two waves in *Little Gidding* (II and V) has a significantly Arnoldian ring;[36] but where he differs from Arnold is that he achieves a full religious explicitness, not in advance of

---

[33] Rudolf Bultmann, *Existence and Faith*, 1964, p. 102 (Fontana edn.).
[34] DS II. st. 2.
[35] See above. p. 64.
[36] Cp. *Stanzas from the Grande Chartreuse*. st. 15, ll. 81–6, and *Obermann*, ll. 74–7.

his poetry, but only as it is successfully realized within it. The poetic activity is itself 'the very powers of growth and production'.[37]

It is this which reminds us of the achievement of the Metaphysicals in such poems as Herbert's *The Collar*, or Donne's *Hymn to God my God in my Sickness*. In each case literary adequacy and theological adequacy seem to be causally related: the presence of the one seeming to ensure the presence of the other. The likeness therefore is more than merely technical; as in a poem by a Metaphysical, so in *Four Quartets*, there is no part of the poem which is not religiously explicit: but each part is so in a different way, and differently for different readers. No 'meaning' could be more explicitly stated than when, in movement IV of *East Coker*, we are told that 'our only health is the disease', and that 'to be restored, our sickness must grow worse'. Some readers may find *Little Gidding* more satisfying than *The Dry Salvages*. Others (as does Dr Leavis) may remain with *Burnt Norton*.

Such diverse holds upon the same experience are the results of what might be called an underlying *theological* grammar, since how we come into the truth of what is asserted is how we continue to hold it as true and certain. In his essay on *Pascal* (1931), and in a later version of the same argument, Eliot speaks of being 'borne gradually, perhaps insensibly . . . by powerful and concurrent reasons' to a position from which an element of faith crystallizes. It is thus that he found himself 'inexorably committed to the dogma of the Incarnation'.[38] Earlier still (1927), he had written of doubt and uncertainty as being 'merely a variety of belief', meaning that faith must take the pressure of doubt and scepticism, if it is to develop adequately into beliefs that can be professed.[39] Assent comes gradually, insensibly, but 'without violence to honesty and nature'. Nevertheless, the order of our encounter with the things of faith may be at odds with the logical order: 'to put the sentiments in order is a later, and an immensely difficult task' (1929).[40]

[37] Coleridge, *BL*, p. 190.

[38] *SE*, p. 408; and *The Listener*, 16 Mar. 1932.

[39] 'Poetry and Belief' and *Notes Towards the Definition of Culture*, pp. 29, 80, 82. See above, p. 111.

[40] 'Second Thoughts about Humanism', *SE*, p. 491; cp. Newman on logic being brought in to arrange 'what no science was employed in gaining' (*Dev.*, p. 176).

That we are reminded of certain key passages in Newman is not a coincidence, if we note the references to Newman in Eliot's published work, and then note which passages from Newman's writing he published in *The Criterion*.[41] 'Powerful and concurrent reasons' is a direct (and acknowledged) reference to the climax of Newman's argument in the *Grammar of Assent*, when he argues that what precipitates the certitude of religious assent are not single arguments of irresistible certainty, but a convergence of probabilities appealing to both the intellect and the imagination, and acting by 'arguments too various for direct enumeration . . ., too powerful and concurrent for refutation', in order, ultimately, to 'elicit one complex act both of inference and of assent'.[42]

To conceive Revelation as being neither light nor darkness, but both together is not a piece of contemporary radical theology, or Eliot in an agnostic phase, but Newman in 1835. In a passage partly published by Eliot in *The Criterion* in 1924, Newman writes:

A revelation is religious doctrine viewed on its illuminated side; a Mystery is the selfsame doctrine viewed on the side unilluminated. *Thus Religious Truth is neither light nor darkness, but both together; it is like the dim view of a country seen in the twilight, with forms half extricated from the darkness, with broken lines and isolated masses.* Revelation, in this way of considering it, is not a revealed *system*, but consists of a number of detached and incomplete truths belonging to a vast system unrevealed, of doctrines and injunctions mysteriously connected together.[43]

Newman's conclusion—that 'considered as a mystery', Revelation is 'a doctrine *lying nid* in language'—perfectly describes Eliot's poetic method, since it is by means of our wrestling with words and meanings that we come into acquaintance with and 'recognize' the fact of the Incarnation: what we hold, we hold as certain, but it remains a truth obscurely revealed. Eliot's omission of the definite article, when he speaks in *Dry Salvages*

[41] See the Appendix, *Eliot and Newman*, p. 130, below.

[42] *GA*, p. 374.

[43] J. H. Newman, *On the Introduction of Rationalistic principles into Revealed Religion* (Tract 73, 1835, *ECH i.* 41–2). Lines between ** are cited by Ramon Fernandez in *The Experience of Newman* published in *The Criterion*, Oct. 1924. In a later work *De la personnalité*, 1928, reviewed by Eliot, Fernandez argues that as, by our actions, we form our personality, so we bring into being the unique means by which our convictions are authenticated. For Newman's view see above, p. 59.

(IV) of Incarnation as 'the gift half-guessed, the gift half under-stood' is significant, since, like Newman, he is taking *the* Incarnation as the general model for the absolute values incarnate in the fully realized human personality. This Newman defines as 'a whole complete in itself, not to be increased by addition, and greater than anything else';[44] and it is in our encounters in common life with this mystery of incarnation that we are led to believe in the reality of what it depends upon—*the* Incarnation of God in Jesus. Since the mind is unequal to its powers of apprehension, we can never successfully acount for these acts of faith and belief. We can only show them. Theory is but the record of what the whole man has already assented to; and since, as Newman remarks, what will convince one person will fail to convince another, for each the way to certitude is perso-nal to him. By 'taking the route you would be likely to take', and by allowing increasing probabilities to converge, you will come to the same place: 'It would be the same at the end of the journey.'[45] It is how, in such conditions, we grow to the explicit certitude of belief that is the subject of *Four Quartets*.

(III) WITHIN THE MAN MADE WHOLE

A dramatic example in our own time of the capacity of the whole man to bring many contradictory things into one is to be seen in the life and death of the theologian Dietrich Bonhoeffer. In theory, his dilemma was that experienced by all the writers so far discussed. He saw himself as having to live through an apparently irreconcilable, polarized conflict between a world 'come of age' and the mythological form of Christianity. He writes:[46]

The movement beginning about the thirteenth century . . . towards the autonomy of man . . . has in our time reached a certain comple-tion. Man has learnt to cope with all questions of importance without recourse to God as a working hypothesis . . . for the last hundred years or so it has been increasingly true of religious questions also.

In a world thus 'come of age' God is not required as a 'working hypothesis', even when we are faced by 'the so-called

[44] This is taken from Newman's description of what it would have been like for a young man to have experienced 'the very presence of Plato' (*Historical Sketches* iii. 41–2).
[45] *LG* I, st. 2.
[46] Dietrich Bonhoeffer, *Letters and Papers from Prison*, 1959, pp. 106–7, 8 June 1944.

ultimate questions—death and guilt'. Yet, Bonhoeffer also opposes himself to all efforts to reduce the mythological elements of Christianity (in the manner of Feuerbach) to an 'essence'; 'I am of the view that the full content, including the mythological concepts, must be maintained.' The mythology is not the 'garb': 'it is the thing itself.'[47]

> There are degrees of perception and degrees of significance, i.e. a *secret* discipline must be re-established whereby the *mysteries* of the Christian faith are preserved from profanation.[48]

Here the similarity between Bonhoeffer and Arnold is very striking. Arnold, too, has his *secret* discipline. It is the 'clerical and respectable Oxford' of Oriel and the Oxford Movement, which had formed him and set his standards in 'morals. . . tone, bearing, and dignity';[49] but he, too, rejects its explicit theological statement as having been superseded. Logically, such contradictory positions are wide open to the kind of criticism so scathingly delivered by Bradley and uneasily repeated by Eliot. Yet to do justice to Bonhoeffer or Arnold as theologians is to see that for them there is never a choice: their calling seems to be, not to resolve such paradoxes, but to live with them. Religion is spoken of as acting out of the future, but understanding out of the past;[50] and Bonhoeffer's tension between a secret discipline and a coming of age is significantly like that between Arnold's two worlds—with the crucial exception that Bonhoeffer's decision was arrived at in the condemned cell. These are the terms on which he was prepared to accept martyrdom—terms which differ very little from those ascribed by Newman to the early Christians: 'In the centre between me and myself, the old and the new existence. . . Here Christ stands', 'reconciling conflicting and divergent descriptions by embodying them in one common representative'.[51]

In this respect, Bonhoeffer's secret is Newman's also—it

---

[47] Ibid., p. 110.

[48] Ibid., p. 95. I have italicized '*secret*'.

[49] *Essays in Criticism*, second series, p. 238.

[50] 'It is perfectly true, as philosophers say, that life must be understood backwards. But they forget the other proposition, that it must be lived forwards' (S. Kierkegaard, *The Journals*, 1843).

[51] The first part of this quotation is from Bonhoeffer, *Lectures on Christology* (1960), E. T. Edwin Robertson, London, 1978, p. 61, and the second part from Newman (*GA*, p. 339).

consists in the unity or personal integrity of a man made whole. Variously described as a tension in unity, or as a poise achieved by delicate discrimination, it is a unity felt as it successfully orders our emotions. It may look like 'oscillation' at a distance, much as the violent commotions of a storm 'do not reach into the depths . . . which are as tranquil and as silent in the storm as in a calm. So it is with the souls of holy men.'[52] In religion it is what the martyrs died to preserve: the unity or integrity which seems to the outsider a perverse paradox, whether it be in Bonhoeffer's practice of a religion in which he no longer 'believed', or in Sir Thomas More's determination to die for a corrupt papacy.

(IV) THE DIFFICULT RESOLUTION

In literature, as in religion, confusion is very easy between *'the solution of the problem and a correct representation of the problem'*, as Chekhov pointed out in a letter.[53] He adds: 'Only the latter is obligatory for the artist. In *Anna Karenina* and *Onegin* not a single problem is solved, but they satisfy you completely just because all their problems are correctly presented.' What is gained is, in Beethoven's phrase, 'the difficult resolution', where the affirmation follows the form of the question so closely that the difference between question and answer may be no more than a tone of voice or in an inflection of idiom: 'Muss es sein? Es muss sein.'[54] It is what may have led Hardy instinctively to conclude the tragedy of *Jude the Obscure* with Job's questionings; and we sense it in the form of Newman's credo in the *Apologia*: *'if* there be a God, *since* there is a God, the human race is implicated in some terrible aboriginal calamity.'[55]

It is a truism of literary criticism that the conditions for achieving imaginative resolution or completion can never be prescribed in advance. Yet this is also true for the resolution of the assent of faith into the explicit certitude of belief. This, too, 'grows out of instincts rather than arguments', and is 'stayed upon a vivid apprehension'.[56] The objects may differ, but the

[52] J. H. Newman, *PPS* v. 69.
[53] *The Selected Letters of Anton Chekhov*, ed. L. Hellman, 1955, p. 57 (27 Oct. 1888).
[54] Cited in Helen Gardner, *Religion and Literature*, London, 1971, p. 34.
[55] *Apo.*, p. 335.
[56] *GA*, p. 163.

form is the same, so that the celebrated words of Coleridge about the imagination can be adapted thus:

Could a rule be given from *without*, *faith* would cease to be *faith*, and sink into a mechanical *belief*. The rules of *faith* are themselves the very powers of growth and production. The *beliefs*, to which they are reducible, present only the outlines and external appearance of the fruit.[57]

If the necessary distinctions between religion and literature are set aside, the religious equivalent of the literary distinction between question and answer is this: the form of the question (conceived, perhaps, as an oscillation between two worlds) is itself an act of faith, and a sign of its presence: it sets the condition which the answers must satisfy, if they are to be held as *living* beliefs. And the further question whether such beliefs are true or false can be resolved only within this framework of polarities and by the activity of the imagination thus engendered: what our beliefs profess must correspond to the forms presented by faith.

Appendix: Eliot and Newman

In addition to the references to Newman in the essays on Pascal and Lancelot Andrewes,[58] Eliot published *The Experience of Newman* by Ramon Fernandez in *The Criterion* for October 1924.[59] I am most grateful to Professor Christopher Ricks for bringing this to my attention.

Fernandez commends Newman for the manner of his distinction between Faith and Reason in the *Oxford University Sermons*, and in the *Grammar of Assent*: Rationalism, his enemy, is ours.[60] The grounds for believing must 'touch the heart',[61] and are not established syllogistically, but grow and converge. They are perceived therefore, not by logical inference, but by 'the illative sense'.[62] Logic is but the ordering subsequently of what we have

---

[57] *Biographia Literaria*, chap. xviii, in the form printed in 1817, ii. 87. 'Could a rule be given from *without*, poetry would cease to be poetry and sink into a mechanical art. the *rules* of the IMAGINATION are themselves the very powers of growth and production. The *words*, to which they are reducible, present only the outlines and external appearance of the fruit.'

[58] *SE* (1969), pp. 341f., 402f.

[59] *The Criterion*, iii. 84–102.

[60] *ECH* i. 42 (quoted in full on p. 126, above).

[61] *Grammar of Assent*, pp. 424–5 (= *GA*, p. 323); *OUS*, pp. 224, 218.

[62] *Grammar of Assent*, p. 347 (= *GA*, pp. 263–4); p. 353 (= *GA*, p. 268).

gained by other means.[63] In thus stressing the creative element in faith, Fernandez goes so far as to assert that belief is a disposition to create what does not yet exist, but is brought into existence by faith. A rejoinder was published by Frederic Manning (*A French Criticism of Newman*).[64] In his reply[65] Fernandez states that 'the believer creates the object of his belief'. Eliot sums up in the same number[66] thus:

M. Fernandez is, from a certain point of view, in closer sympathy with Newman than are many of Newman's Christian or literary apologists; he is in much closer sympathy with Newman in his place and *time*: with Newman, in fact—and it is a large part—in so far as Newman was *not* Christian or Catholic. He does not understand, perhaps, that in which Newman believed or tried to believe, but he understands, better than almost anyone, *the way in which* Newman believed or tried to believe it.[67]

II. Continuity and Discontinuity

Religious imagination experiences a mystery which can never be reduced to a consistent or general theory: we worship a loving God, yet one who tolerates undeserved suffering:

> Our only health is the disease
> If we obey the dying nurse
> Whose constant care is not to please
> But to remind of our, and Adam's curse,
> And that, to be restored, our sickness must grow worse.

We also assume that beneath the duality there exists a coherent and unified presence. How does the object of faith succeed in perpetuating its identity through change? This question is complicated by the fact that although the polarizing tendency of religious imagination may make for excellent drama in play, parable, and novel, it does not readily suggest how traditional beliefs may be handed on to a new and different generation, or how they may be adapted to circumstances radically changed from those in which they originated. Yet, as we have seen, this

---

[63] *Development of Christian Doctrine*, p. 190 (= *Dev.*, p. 176).
[64] Jan. 1926, *The Criterion*, iv. 19–31.
[65] *The Criterion*, iv. 645–58.
[66] Ibid., pp. 751–7.
[67] Ibid., p. 753.

polar or 'paratactic' quality has characterized the expression of religious sensibility from earliest times. It was still acceptable to Shakespeare and Andrewes; it lingered in Russia until the Revolution. It is what, in our own times, Eliot has restored particularly in *Four Quartets* and, as I have argued, it is the form in which religious imagination persists through the nineteenth century and after.

But, as Newman shows, it is present in the experience of Christians from the start in the event of the Incarnation, which 'reconciles conflicting and divergent descriptions'—that the Messiah could both suffer, yet be victorious, and his people be both the children of Abraham, yet 'sinners of the Gentiles'.[68] Thus, in religion, we seem to be committed to conceiving our faith in ways which express how what is ambiguous, even paradoxical, succeeds in being held in a unifying focus. So far this has been variously described as a 'meeting', a saying and unsaying, a correction by opposite strokes, as diverse functions seeking equilibrium, or the effort to see stereoscopically. I use the term 'polarity' to denote this appearance of contradiction which, although irreducible verbally, conceptually, or logically, neither stands for an irresolvable dualism in experience, nor calls into question the underlying unity of or wholeness of that experience. It is what is expressed when we speak of the one God who comprises the Three persons of the Trinity, or of the warfare of God and Satan.

I choose to use the 'polar' form as crucial since it brings out the essentially dialectical movement within tradition, which we experience initially, as Coleridge notes and as Arnold deplores, as a suspension between permanence (continuity with the past) and revolutionary change (anticipation of the future). All innovators bring something out of the past, at present neglected, and show how it enables us to live more fully in the present, and how identity is thus perpetuated or conserved by change. Eliot returned to the seventeenth century and to the Metaphysical poets to bring out the qualities which an authentic contemporary poetic idiom required, and Newman returned to the Fathers for his revolutionary claim that the laity should be 'consulted' by the church hierarchy. Each, in his way, saw that what provokes the movement its opponents condemn as revolu-

[68] *GA*, p. 339.

tionary change is the effort of a powerful imagination to bring
alive the values and beliefs it starts from in the tradition it has
inherited. Thus to experience the pain and tension of being
between two worlds does not necessarily signalize a radical
discontinuity: it may be the precondition for discerning with
exactitude what needs to be conserved.

To speak of this experience, as does Arnold, as one of dissociation may spring from confusing custom with tradition. In a
time of rapid change, customs are quickly superseded, and their
imposition becomes increasingly implausible. We should distinguish, however, between customs (which are imposed) and
tradition (which is realized). This, in turn, derives from a
distinction between faith and beliefs, where unity of faith implies, not a uniformity of customs and beliefs, but their diversity
within a common tradition.

Uniformity of belief differs from the unity of faith within
tradition for the same reason that the rudimentary language of
dogma differs from conceptual definitions systematically imposed. What has enabled us to see this is that we live at the end
of three centuries of triumphant and (for churchmen) largely
unconscious rationalism, in which our former emphasis upon
systematic formulations concealed the essential (and ancient)
plurality of tradition. We are once more beginning to see that
conceptual errors and epistemological mistakes are not sufficient evidence of loss of faith, or grounds for excommunica-
tion, and that heresy is chiefly (and anciently) a matter of
imbalance or excess, a single-minded 'picking and choosing', or
a 'disowning and protesting against other truth, which they
fancy *inconsistent* with it'.[69]

Thus the enemy of tradition has always been what Blake calls
'single vision', by which he means the suppression of conflicting
points of view, if these appear to be 'discontinuous' with inherited customs and beliefs. This overlooks the fact that logical
sequence may be but the subsequent 'paper record' of the
development of mind, as Newman remarks; since, as Lawrence
also reminds us, to bring our minds to bear upon deeply held
convictions is to think and feel 'at the same time' and, in doing
so, 'the mind makes curious swoops and circles'. And we are

[69] Newman, *Select Treatises of St. Athanasius*, ii. 450, note (my italics)–a conclusion also
emphasized by Victor White, *Soul and Psyche*, p. 279, n. 54.

reminded of the method of *Four Quartets*, when Lawrence notes the 'curious spiral rhythm' as 'the mind approaches again and again the point of concern, repeats itself, goes back, destroys the time-sequence entirely'.[70]

It is for reasons such as these that the forms expressive of tradition, in early times and before rationalism dominated European sensibility, were eikons or symbols. These, as they hold diverse beliefs in an equilibrium of resolved tension, *show* unity: how Christ is both God and man is shown in the eikon of the Virgin and Child. Equally ancient and equally imaginative is that conception of tradition as being 'the greatest multiplicity in the deepest possible unity'.[71] This, von Hügel's definition, is even more richly conceived by the nineteenth-century Russian theologians, including Dostoevsky, as 'sobornost', which is defined by Khomiakov as 'L'unité dans la pluralité . . . l'unanimité libre'.[72] Such a conception is regained as we become aware of the distinction between faith and beliefs, and of the unity of faith as being compatible with diversity of belief. It is what forms ecumenical methodology, and is the source of our conviction that we can, in a *new* way, become one in Christ.

What, however, is the guarantee against diversity turning into dissociation and sectarianism? Within Catholic tradition belief in diversity has always presupposed a pre-existing unity. Medieval people believed that this could be explicitly stated and realized. For us, however, such unity is implicit, and, if expressible, only with difficulty. The reclaiming of an old word, 'sobornost', is not only a means of renewing our understanding of the more familiar synonym, 'catholic'. It also re-creates our understanding of the papacy, for example, by changing the focus from imposing and pronouncing to witnessing, standing, or signifying in the sacramental and symbolic sense, to the unity implicit in a growing diversity. This, in the sense used above, is an eikonographic function. By protecting 'legitimate differences, while at the same time assuring that such differences do not hinder unity but rather contribute toward it',[73] the pope partakes of the reality, or unity, he makes intelligible. The chief

[70] *Phoenix*, selections, ed. A. H. Inglis, Penguin Books, 1971, p. 265.

[71] Von Hügel, *The Mystical Element of Religion*, London, 1923, i. 66–7.

[72] 'Lettre au rédacteur de l'Union Chrétienne, à l'occasion d'un discours du Père Gagarine, Jésuite' (1860), in *L'Eglise Latine*, Lausanne, 1872, p. 398.

[73] *Lumen Gentium*, paragraph 13.

form of future papal service, therefore, may be to stand for the unity, not merely of Catholics, or even of Christians, but of all men, the pope's function being to maximize unity through the whole world, so that *all* may be one in Christ.

It is significant to notice to what extent theologians (under pressure of the movement towards a new unity in Christ) increasingly conceive tradition in polar form. Yves Congar, for example, notes how the teaching about salvation is delivered in two forms and according to two modes. The Church both continues the Jewish *torah* and yet is a new dispensation. Why, he asks,[74] is there always a positive and negative pole in the two Testaments, or between Law and Grace? Could this be a sign that one reality must always be complemented in another, and by another; and that at the heart of reality there exists a structure of things based upon duality in unity, agreement and completeness in difference?

Other theologians also conceive tradition as polarized between what Jean-Louis Leuba calls 'two different, yet conjugated, modes: that of the institution and that of the event'.[75] This is akin to von Hügel's interaction between 'this-worldliness' and 'other-worldliness',[76] or (in a slightly different sense) to Péguy's between 'la politique' and 'la mystique'.

It is of great significance that Coleridge's way of describing the action of imagination in terms of the polarized magnetic field applies exactly to this conception of tradition, since this apprehension of polarity, where we cannot conceive the poles without conceiving the special relation between them, is for Coleridge the basic act of imagination.[77] To conceive tradition in terms of a magnetic field, whose essential characteristic is an opposed relation between negative and positive poles, helps us to grasp its plural structure yet its essentially unitary operation. But it also helps us to to understand continuity and development in a different way.

[74] Y. Congar, *Tradition and Traditions*, E. T., London, 1966, pp. 374–5; 455.

[75] In *'L'Institution et L'Événement'*, *Les Deux Modes de l'oeuvre de Dieu selon le Nouveau Testament, leur différence, leur unité*, 1950, E.T. *New Testament Pattern*, London, 1953, p. 127. A similar claim—that the divine activity requires contrasting explanations which are neither reducible nor assimilable to each other—is made by F. W. Dillistone in *The Structure of the Divine Society*, 1951.

[76] See above, p. 113

[77] *BL*, p. 151; *CN* 4326.

When it is assumed that continuity within tradition requires us to assume the development of our beliefs to be an evolutionary process, blandly broadening on from precedent to precedent, as it were, then evidence of discontinuity (where it can be provided) is fatal. This was certainly the view of many theologians in the nineteenth century, and alone among them, Newman felt the pressure of development of doctrine and belief for what we now see it to be: a necessity forced upon us, often unpleasant and unwelcome, and arising from our own inadequacies, and certainly not an agreeable transition to be sought after and enjoyed. It may sometimes be a penalty rather than a reward.[78] If we fail to relativize the present, we become deceived by the chronology of belief, since what comes later in time is not necessarily a development. It may be an impoverishment or a corruption.

Conversely, the present state of religious faith and practice may become, by 1984, the future's 'faded song'. And this may be the reason why each new generation often seems 'improperly' conservative to its elders as, in order to establish its own engagement with tradition, it revives what had seemed to be superseded as emblematic of the bad old days. This, to the new generation, becomes 'a faded song', or subject 'of wistful regret for those who are not yet here to regret'.[79] The Oxford Movement, for example, revived the superseded Fathers of the Church, as the Romantics resurrected the discredited architecture of the middle ages. They did not so much use or refer to the past as perceive it differently and, in doing so, they came to hold a different perception of the whole tradition from their elders. The experience of radical change, therefore, marks the claim of a tradition upon us, and not our failure to engage with it. The claim is felt initially as a jump or discontinuity, which we do not so much welcome as suffer, 'placing the mind [as Coleridge remarks] in an angry state'.[80] We have seen it focused in such

---

[78] 'a change in theological teaching involves either the commission or the confession of sin; it is either the profession or the renunciation of erroneous doctrine, and if it does not succeed in proving the fact of past guilt, it, *ipso facto*, implies present. In other words, every change in religion carries with it its own condemnation, which is not attended by deep repentance' (*Tract XC*, in J. H. Newman, *Via Media*, ii. 270.)

[79] See above, pp. 210ff., for Eliot's treatment of this theme.

[80] *CN* 2907.

dilemmas as: is God an adjective or a noun? What distinctions between faith and belief are required if we are to do justice to the unity we now experience as Christians? When customary teaching is inconsistent with new facts, by what authority does the present alter the past?

To put questions in so flat a form, however, is to forget the primacy of imagination, and that it is literary criticism, for example, which shows us how to detect whether 'God' is being used correctly to denote something more than either a mental projection or a cliché. It also shows how a form may preserve its identity, yet provoke unceasing reinterpretation; and how such a working of imagination both depends upon a trustworthy social framework and is creative of it. What we seek is not simple answers to simple questions, but how to frame those questions. Is it true that we can neither live with Christianity as it is, nor live without it? And, if so, are our beliefs saving facts, or saving lies? How, in other words, does the Christian story continue to partake of the reality it renders intelligible?

We are repeating Newman's discovery when we realize that what we are seeking is nothing so dramatic as the epigenesis, metamorphosis, or transvaluation of belief. Instead, our aim is 'the difficult resolution', where what is asserted imaginatively is the form or order of the question, to which a solution must be adequate if it is to be entertained or professed as a belief.[81] And it is only as we allow ourselves to experience the pain, tension, crucifixion, of discovery and change that we can truly discern what needs to be conserved. The function of the 'new' conviction or belief is to provoke the assertion of the old, but thereby to place it in a new order: 'Great good, therefore, of such revolution as alters, not by exclusion, but by an enlargement that includes the former, though it places it in a new point of view.'[82] Or, to use the familiar words of T. S. Eliot, 'the past (is) altered by the present as much as the present is directed by the past'. The effect of development is to alter 'the *whole* existing order . . ., if ever so slightly'.

[81] See above, p. 129, for the remark by Chekhov that in *Anna Karenina* and *Onegin*, 'not a single problem is solved, but they satisfy you completely just because all their problems are correctly presented'. This also applies to Turgenev's treatment of the relation between parents and children discussed below, p. 152.

[82] Coleridge, *CN* 2907.

Applied to religion and to the development of doctrine this view has some interesting consequences: development is no longer conceived to be a mere matter of logical sequence, but in Tyrrell's words it may be conceived as a process 'of active reconstruction'.[83] The experience of discontinuity, far from being incompatible with tradition, may be a precondition for our authentic engagement with it. As Newman asserted,[84] to live within a tradition is not to live by a single criterion; instead, it is to live at the centre of a potential conflict, as each aspect of the tradition attempts to become the master. Equilibrium, when achieved, is always at risk. The bringing of our beliefs into relation with changed circumstances, like the emergence of convictions into authentic beliefs, will often appear to be hesitant, even timid. The certitude it expresses may appear to be at once interrogative and persistent. These words, used by Donald Mackinnon of Bishop Bell's manner in opposing area bombing during the war, raise an echo. It is of the Pauline paradox—that we are deceivers, yet true, sorrowful, yet always rejoicing.[85] What is the significance of this echo, and of Paul's hesitation? I would suggest that it may be that Paul, too, in seeking to articulate his beliefs, finds that he is committed to the painful labour, not only of bringing old, worn out, smooth words back to life, but of so modifying and developing them as to use them in a new sense.

The signal of success is when what was experienced, for example, as an opposition between two worlds, or between past beliefs and present needs, is at last resolved into a new harmony. The phrase used by Newman to describe the development of doctrine—that it is a translation into a new language—finds a parallel in Eliot's description of the poet's task as being to dislocate the language into meaning, and in Wallace Stevens's assertion that 'progress in any aspect is a movement through changes of terminology'.

What is assumed is the continuity of the language which

[83] 'I gather wild flowers as I go along, and arrange them each moment, according to what I have got in hand, in some sort of harmonious unity. I gather more, and forthwith I break up the unity in favour of another more inclusive arrangement, which takes in all the old materials in new relations. . . . It is not a process of passive unfolding, but of active reconstruction' (*Essays on Faith and Immortality*, London, 1914, p. 127).

[84] See above, pp. 70, 80.

[85] 2 Cor. 6:8.

must be learned before it can be modified; and this is precisely the chief meaning of 'tradition' in the religious or the literary sense. For the poet it is the renewal of metaphor which brings the truth home to us. Thus, besides speaking of language as an armoury of past trophies and future weapons, he can speak of the powers of conscious intellect as being increased 'by the accession of an organon or new word', or by using old words in a new sense[86]—as Eliot's poetry testifies. If we succeed, we no longer stand simply between two worlds: each has become much like the other:

> But, as the passage now presents no hindrance
> To the spirit unappeased and peregrine
> Between two worlds become much like each other,
> So I find words I never thought to speak
> In streets I never thought I should revisit
> When I left my body on a distant shore.
>
> *(Little Gidding* II)

The theologian, too, has to reclaim theological language from its inherent tendency to remain a 'projection' or to degenerate into clichés: 'God', and 'conscience', but also 'consult', 'sobornost', and even 'contraception'—how are we to understand these words? Like the poet, the theologian has to say and unsay to a positive result. In each case the integrity sought, if it is achieved, is signalized by technical or linguistic accomplishment,[87] since as the poetry of Wordsworth and Eliot shows, it is within the successful poetic evocation of the experience that its meaning lies hidden. We cannot be told directly what has happened (when we say, for example, that we have come to believe that God was incarnate in Jesus) only how it has happened; but the *how*, when it is convincingly evoked, tells us *what*.[88] For example, in describing what other poets have called a moment of vision, or an unattended moment, Wordsworth speaks of that 'recognition of glory',

---

[86] Coleridge, *BL*, p. 159, *CN* 3268, 3660.

[87] Eliot, in writing of Blake, remarks: 'This honesty never exists without great technical accomplishment' (*SE*, p. 317)–a judgement applied to Eliot's own poetry by Dr Leavis (*New Bearings in English Poetry*, London, 1932, p. 119).

[88] See above, p. 123.

> —when the light of sense
> Goes out, but with a flash that has revealed
> The invisible world.[89]

This is to see, as if and for the moment, 'stereoscopically'. It is gained by that facility in metaphor which, as the poet hovers between images, leaves 'a middle state of mind more strictly appropriate to the imagination than any other'.[90] It is the same for the theologian, as when Kierkegaard writes that:

> to believe means precisely that dialectical *hovering* which, although in fear and trembling, never despairs; faith is an infinite self-made care as to whether one has faith—and that self-made care is faith.[91]

It is the poet who shows the theologian how to prevent his beliefs from ossifying into 'big-words', by showing him the method by which we avoid cliché and secure meaning. As for the poet, so for the theologian, Revelation is a 'doctrine lying hid in language' in a way comparable to that in which Shakespeare's intention is hidden in the dynamic structure of *Lear* or *Hamlet*, whose meaning we grasp only in so far as we attend to the play as a whole and to the complete range of metaphor it convincingly realizes and orders. But besides being a doctrine hid in language, Revelation is also the Word, once spoken in a context long since vanished ('Christ wrote only in the sand', as Blondel remarks), and now grasped only as it is trustworthily renewed, that is translated, developed, and secularized in ever-new contexts and changing cultures. Developments do not have to be engineered: they happen, as the living power within Christianity continues to modify itself into what can still 'be believed in '.[92] How we assess or authenticate developments is by a method which, propounded by Newman as a theologian, is yet essentially literary. A true development returns us to the rudimentary dogmas and signs of tradition as we return to a great Shakespearean tragedy—each re-reading of *Hamlet*, for example, leads to a reinterpretation of the *whole* play.[93] What matters is not that successive interpretations should form a

---

[89] *The Prelude*, vi. 600f.
[90] Coleridge, *Shakespearean Criticism*, ed. T. M. Raysor, London, 1960, ii. 103.
[91] *Journals*, Oxford, 1939, p. 763 (my italics).
[92] Eliot, see above, p. 111.
[93] See above, pp. 25f.

simple logical sequence, but that our present interpretation should be more and not less adequate to the text than its predecessors.

For example, as we realize how far the ecclesiastical conceptions of women rested less upon scripture and more upon custom, so the Marian dogmas of the nineteenth century, which had the conscious intention of reaffirming the status of Mary in order to emphasize the divinity of her son in the face of Liberal Protestant devaluation, may be seen increasingly as unconscious anticipations of the changed status of women. They may serve as the source for developments of a radical kind in our understanding of women, not merely in marriage, but in the ministry of the Church. But what is significant is the widespread assumption that such new questions (especially about contraception and family size) should be justified as developments of tradition—further evidence that talk of radical discontinuity may, like talk of radical doubt, be a philosophical invention.

In religion the 'Great Divide' may itself also be an invention. It is we who have created it, since directly we bring together the two chief writers discussed in this book—the poet and the theologian—we see to what extent the oscillations which, for Arnold and Hardy, are signs of a dissociation and radical discontinuity, are for Eliot and Newman but the signs preparatory to a mutation. They are the form of the question to which a development of doctrine (or belief) is the answer. But we have also seen to what extent this is so because they stand explicitly within a tradition which embraces Augustine, Anselm, and Pascal. To exercise imagination, not outside the Christian faith, but within it, is what enables them to be certain that they will see the present in focus with the past; and as the two worlds become 'much like each other', so the end of all our exploring

> Will be to arrive where we started
> And know the place for the first time.

PART THREE

THE CONSEQUENCES FOR THEOLOGY
AND LITERARY CRITICISM

5

Inhibitions

(1) LITERARY

The argument of this book is that the real assent we make to the
primary forms of religious faith (expressed in metaphor, symbol, and story) is of the same kind as the imaginative assent we
make to the primary forms of literature. In the articulation of
this assent the theologian and the literary critic share what I
have referred to as a common grammar, if by grammar is
understood that underlying form or structure which is revealed
as we learn and use a language. The purpose of this book has
been to show to what extent such a grammar common to
literature and religion still exists. If this is so, what effect ought
its existence to have on theology on the one hand and on literary
criticism on the other? Current practice is still to accept as
inevitable a more radical disjunction of our predispositions.
How far we are prepared to go—whether we stop short at poetic
faith, or go on to religious belief—is usually regarded as merely
a matter of choice, since it is assumed that all that literature can
arouse and its criticism elucidate is 'that willing suspension of
disbelief which constitutes poetic faith'.[1] By rightly formulating
the questions, literary art may disclose an order *in* reality, but
that is all. The poet can do no more than 'hope it might be so'.
To be able to believe that it is so is to make 'a firm assent' to
beliefs, however 'obscurely revealed'—and for this Virgil must
leave us: we need other guides.[2] The task of authenticating that
order and the convictions it reveals is for theologians and
philosophers.

The risk is, as we have seen, that we shall look for the wrong
kind of proof—that of simple and clear demonstration, so that
we shall spend fifty fruitless years 'looking for God', as did
Hardy; or, like Raskolnikov,[3] we shall first require a satisfactory
theory of life before giving ourselves to life, by requiring the

---

[1] *BL*, p. 147.
[2] See above, p. 87.
[3] Dostoevsky, *Crime and Punishment*, E.T. Penguin, 1966, pp. 467, 471.

objects of faith to be rationally verified before they may be affirmed. This is to ask for the iron bar of logical demonstration when circumstances permit only the woven cable of probabilities. It is to condemn ourselves to what is described by Hardy, Arnold, and others in such cognate metaphors as those of snakes lying side by side, of rams butting each other, and of wanderers between a past dead faith and a future unborn belief. It is to be in a condition where we can neither live with religion as it is, nor live without it. This is also the fate of Stephen Dedalus who remains paralysed between two worlds, or of those who, waiting for Godot, expect not a vision but a nightmare. Psychologically, this comes close to the classical definition of a neurosis as a state of chronic indecision or fixation. We can be freed from such inhibitions only as we see our difficulty as arising, not from radical doubt, but from failing to find our proofs.

Our inhibitions can arise from undervaluing the beliefs already implicit in our imaginative assents. George Eliot, Matthew Arnold, and Thomas Hardy, for example, were unable simply to profess inherited and traditional beliefs; but their imagination kept alive what their reason could no longer explain or profess. Beliefs may die, but faith survives, like an ember, within imagination. Seen thus, novels and poems are forms of faith which invite theological investigation—but with the proviso that their integrity as imaginative forms is rigorously observed. Their significance can be correctly interpreted only as we succeed in preventing the over-zealous assimilation of literary criticism to theology. Bridges there may be, but they must be discovered rather than engineered. Even so, when bridges are revealed they must be crossed. It is harmful to remain unaware of the extent to which our real and imaginative assents have already committed us to their authentication. Without knowing it, we can be out over 70,000 fathoms and already *en voyage*. We see this only when we are deprived of the way of life to which our imagination has committed us—by revolution, bereavement, or more simply by old age. Then we realize explicitly, but too late, what, implicitly, we had come to believe. And Newman's warning is salutary: we were mistaken to suppose that we had been imprisoned in Doubting Castle.

(II) THEOLOGICAL

From the standpoint of theology, the inhibitions which prevent us from discovering and using the common grammar are deep and serious. As we have seen, the theologian may hold to outworn and outmoded beliefs, ignoring the imaginative pressure to make them credible or to transform them, from a sense of pastoral prudence: it is *safer* to believe the old things in the old way. But in the sixteenth and seventeenth centuries, as Coleridge and Maurice point out, it was polemical rather than pastoral considerations which encouraged theologians to show an overweening confidence in their theological explanations—at the cost of imaginative responsiveness. In the nineteenth century, as the Modernists discovered, the difficulty was to bring the dogmatic, or rudimentary, forms of religious belief into accord with the experience of what seemed to be a uniquely modern way of life. To safeguard the dogmas the papacy inhibited their explanation; and, as Loisy remarked, the answers were provided before the questions had been formulated. What was worse was that the good faith of the questioners was itself put into question. Readiness to convict the critic of unbelief is the most dangerous consequence of a religion divorced from imagination, since it is only when the questions have been correctly formulated, and thus made a fit subject for a 'real' assent, that the work of authentication may safely be begun. The only 'safe' theology is that which feels the agony of Dmitry Karamazov's cry that 'God sets us nothing but riddles'.[4]

The most serious source of theological inhibition, however, arises when the language of religion appears to be no longer that of the secular culture, and when its words, as they fall out of general use, become meaningless—the sentiments they stand for fading with them. The common grammar may then seem plausible only within a vanished culture. The Great War, for example, intensified what the Industrial Revolution had revealed. While the degree of obedience which enabled men to die in the mud of Passchendaele testified to the strength of their

---

[4] Dostoevsky. *The Brothers Karamazov*. p. 123.

moral and religious convictions,[5] as the war dragged on, so the language of such convictions was felt to be a rhetoric without power to affect the motives for social and political action, and the common grammar seemed to be that of a dead language. The battle-fields of the Somme forced the same conclusion upon an entire generation as that which Feuerbach had reached three-quarters of a century before: that we can neither live with our religious beliefs as they are, nor live without them.

These are real enough sources of inhibition; but to claim that they invalidate the order or process by which we move from faith to belief is to be deceived by what I have called the chronology of belief. When T. S. Eliot succeeds in associating faith and belief, imagination and religion, he does so by the same methods and in the same way as Newman a century earlier. Each discovers a grammar whose principles and structure are the same, and by means of which faith and belief become compatible—as they do for Bonhoeffer, in the manner of his life and death. And when such compatibility is achieved, and as, afterwards, we put the sentiments in order, we discover that although the chronological order (or order in which we exercise imaginative, rational, or ethical responses to the claims of a religion) varies with individuals, circumstances, and cultural assumptions, the logical order remains what it always has been.

Those who are deceived by the chronology of belief are inhibited from appreciating the significance of overlapping forms and methods. Literary criticism is never strictly aesthetic, any more than religious beliefs are strictly religious, or secularity strictly secular. Although interdisciplinary tendencies should be prudently managed, since unconscious and easy assimilations destroy the very responses they refer to, so also do inhibitions; and Wittgenstein's warning against inhibiting such responses is equally necessary: that it is how a term is used in other disciplines (or language games) that determines its *sense*

---

[5] 'This Western-front business couldn't be done again. . . . This took religion and years of plenty and tremendous sureties and the exact relation that existed between the classes . . . you had to have a whole-souled sentimental equipment going back further than you could remember. . . . There was a century of middle-class love spent here'. (Scott FitzGerald, *Tender is the Night*, 1953, the Bodley Head edn. of Scott Fitzgerald, vol. ii, the original version of 1934, 3rd impression 1973, Book One, xiii. 67–8).

in its own discipline (or language game). It certainly determines its reality.[6]

The relation between faith and belief in general, and poetic faith and religious belief in particular, is peculiarly one of overlap, since in defining one term we find ourselves implying the other: belief is not only where we end, it may be where we begin; and faith cannot be expressed except in terms of its *implicit* beliefs. Yet the distinction remains essential if what is imaginatively credible is to preserve its creative character, on the one hand, and if the deliberative character of belief is to be safeguarded, on the other. Faith is in what is alive; belief in what is true—a distinction akin to Kierkegaard's between spontaneity and reflection. Yet, as we read Shakespeare or Dostoevsky and strive to keep imagination separate from belief, and conviction from authentication, so we feel their overlapping pressure, their urge to 'modulate into each other'.[7] Literature is careless of exact boundaries—'nice customs curtsy to great kings'—and it is a mark of greatness in literature when a work contains more than is needed, and the author achieves more than he consciously intends. Lawrence's advice is just, therefore: never trust the author, trust the tale. We see this in George Eliot's treatment of religion: it is so much wider and deeper than its origins in Feuerbach and Strauss; as is Dostoevsky's treatment of the religious ideas of his theological mentor, Vladimir Solovyev, in *The Brothers Karamazov*.

This is what it is to 'realize' the resources of a language, and it is precisely in dealing with this question—what it is to realize to the full the resources of the language—that theology and literary criticism find common ground, and require most mutual support.

[6] L. Wittgenstein, *Remarks on the Foundation of Mathematics*, 1956, iv, 2, 133.
[7] Hardy, see above, p. 108.

Overlapping Questions

(1) THE RESOURCES OF A LANGUAGE

Of all forms of continuity, the most obstinate are those which are apparent in the preservation of a language. What is it, then, for the resources of a language to be fully realized? In a negative sense, as is shown by a comparison of the enriched Shakespearean metaphors with the translucent metaphors of a later poet like Arnold, a language which drops any of its sources grows thinner, loses a dimension, or suffers a diminished range of reference. A public language is as rich as the sources from which it is derived; and it has dimensions to the extent that the rules for its use are a function of its history. But is this to say more than Coleridge who, quoting Dante, conceives a language to contain at once the trophies of its past, and the weapons (or means) of its future conquests?[1] A metaphor (like a proposition) succeeds as it *shows* reality: reality is what its form 'models'; and to speak of a 'mere' metaphor, or 'placebo', is to imply some kind of failure or even deception. It is also to refer somewhat too loosely to a metaphor's fading or being so 'translucent' as to become a mere simile or allegory. As Dr Johnson remarked of the metaphysical poets, metaphor is what happens when 'the most heterogeneous ideas are yoked by violence together'.[2] Donne, for example, ends one of his *Holy Sonnets* by claiming that he will never be free unless he is 'enthralled' by God, 'Nor ever chast, except you ravish mee'—an example which illustrates how, by emphasizing unlikeness and discontinuity, metaphor dislocates customary usage in order to create new meaning. Eliot, for example, uses the analogy of illness to sin to create a metaphor of a mental condition which must grow worse before it may be cured; and in *The Dry Salvages*, by yoking the conflicting meanings of 'salvage' and 'savage' he is able to

---

[1] *BL*, chap. xvi. It is interesting to note that Marcuse regards the suppression of this 'historical' dimension in everyday speech as one of the factors which confine man to the single dimensional or closed technological society. See H. Marcuse, *One Dimensional Man*, London, 1968, pp. 86, 147.

[2] Samuel Johnson, *Lives of the Poets*, i. 14.

suggest that, as we are 'savaged' by God, so we are 'salvaged'.[3]

To dismiss all ancient words, therefore, as metaphors lacking an objectively ascertainable content—to treat 'God' as simply an adjective and 'conscience' as merely the expression of an emotion—is to accept too little from what a persistent metaphor has to offer. It is to fail to grasp Coleridge's distinction between allegory and analogue (deriving as this does from the more celebrated distinction between fancy and imagination),[4] or Newman's between assents which evaporate and those which endure.[5] Metaphors are effective in proportion to their complexity, and although they become in general less dense after Shakespeare and the Metaphysical writers, to assume that density of metaphor is a characteristic peculiar to literature before 1688, and that a change of consciousness and culture prevents its reappearance is to be deceived by the chronology of metaphor. Density of metaphor continues to be successfully realized, but more often by novelists (such as Dickens) than by poets (such as Arnold). In the nineteenth century it is the novel which increasingly performs the function of dramatic poetry. Metaphor, in its extended form as story or myth, continues to be the form which most adequately expresses beliefs and values. Thus, in speaking of a character in a Lawrence story as having chosen life, Dr Leavis asserts that how life has been chosen requires the whole form of the story to define; but in defining it, the story justifies that way of describing the decision. In such circumstances, it remains true that to perceive is to mythologize, since the only way in which we can fully explain or justify our values and beliefs is to tell a story. Hence the persistence of stories and myths as various as those of Icarus, Daedalus, Job, and Prometheus. Not only do they recur, they occur in widely differing cultures, as Jung remarks. Such stories, by their persistence and successful recurrence, perform the classic task of imagination: they dissipate and destroy single-mindedness[6] and substitute for single vision diverse levels of never-ending interpretation. As we engage with them, so they extend the range of our capacities: they search us out; they 'find' us. They

---

[3] See above, p. 119: *EC* IV and *DS* II.
[4] See p. 28 above.
[5] See p. 54 above.
[6] See above, p. 73, n. 94.

are frameworks of reference within which we grow out of ourselves. Can we, in fact, visualize a culture in which *Lear* and *Macbeth* could no longer be performed? Likewise the parables. They, too, possess this literary power to rouse the faculties of man to act, by calling us out of a world grown too smoothly familiar, and inviting us to move around in worlds unrecognized. Coleridge equates poetry and religion with sickness and sorrow as 'The Extenders of Consciousness', adding, 'The truth is, we stop in the sense of Life just when we are not *forced* to go on—and then adopt a permission of our feelings for a precept of our Reason.'[7] This reinforces what the *Four Quartets* express—that we do not move willingly out over 70,000 fathoms, or happily accept that there is more to our experience than the well-adjusted present requires.

In its simplest form, a successful metaphor gives us a shock, helping us, thereby, to adapt to a changed reality. Thus, Turgenev conceives the changed relationships between generations, between parents and children, as one between a fungus and a falcon—metaphors pointing to a distinction which, felt as one of kind or quality (between a plant and a bird) is also one of relationship (both are organisms).[8] The irony is that they are like one another, and yet even in this resemblance unlike. But for the parents to see their son thus marks a change also in themselves and in their relationship: they now cling to each other as never before, 'not even in their youth'.

It is the connection between the sign and the thing signified which remains the mystery. Like 'signals'[9] from 'worlds not recognized', they come spontaneously but obliquely. What they seem to demonstrate conclusively is that there are other 'frameworks' of experience than the empirical, that is, than what we can see clearly and distinctly in front of our eyes. These experiences come like invitations; they cannot be consciously willed, but come to what Hardy calls a 'self unseeing':

[7] *CN* 3632.

[8] 'A son is an independent person. He's like a falcon that comes when he wills and flies off when he lists; but you and I are like the funguses growing in a hollow tree: here we sit side by side, not budging an inch. It is only I who will stay with you always, faithful for ever, just as you will stay with me' (Turgenev, *Fathers and Sons*, E.T. Penguin, 1965, p. 163). See the discussion above of analogy on pp. 28f.

[9] See Peter Berger, *A Rumour of Angels*, Penguin 1971, pp. 64, 70, for the argument that the sociologist is obliged to accept the existence in 'ordinary everyday awareness' of 'signals of transcendence. . . which challenge the empirical framework'.

> Childlike, I danced in a dream;
> Blessing emblazoned that day;
> Everything glowed with a gleam;
> Yet we were looking away!

These are the moments in which the focus of our attention changes unconsciously and spontaneously.[10] What we experience, we experience obliquely, and if it has a pattern it is one perceived in rare moments of inattention.[11] And, furthermore, it is recollected: it is recognized for what it is only in retrospect. and in retrospect it appears to have been the perception of value, of 'transcendent' value. As Edward Thomas says:

> We imagined that happiness
> Was something different
> And this was something less.

Elsewhere I have suggested that this is what Wordsworth intends when, in *The Prelude*, he writes of 'spots of time'.[12] In Edward Thomas such 'spots' are often recognized in a sudden flash of irony, as when he ends a poem:

> Some day I shall think this a happy day.

What is significant is that it is the signals that lend themselves to irony—the negative signals (of humour and damnation), rather than the positives (of hope and order), whose 'transcendent' reference is now most acceptable and socially plausible. Rarely passionate in its affirmations, ours is a society which finds it easier to be wry and ironic; but irony, the friend of belief, is almost as much the enemy of faith as of fanaticism: it belongs to the surface of faith, not to its depths; to polite literature, not to liturgy. And it could be a significant sign of restricted sensibility, if it is only the joker who is permitted to arouse the sense of the supernatural. Yet Waiting for Godot is as old as Bottom's Dream—and older:

[10] See *Philosophical Investigations* for Wittgenstein's reference (p. 645) to the difficulty of pinning an aspect down, because directly it is pinned down, it seems to vanish or to change into something else: 'It is as if one had altered the adjustment of a microscope.' This is an excellent description of our response to a Shakespearean tragedy like *Lear*: we are continually having to change focus: at all times the perceptual field is much less simple than we had supposed.

[11] T. S. Eliot, *SE*, p. 232.

[12] See my *Newman and the Common Tradition*, pp. 27ff., and the discussion above, p. 123.

Methought I was, and methought I had. . . . The eye of man hath
not heard, the ear of man hath not seen, man's hand is not able to
taste, his tongue to conceive, nor his heart to report, what my dream
was.

To discover the other pole of the irony, we are obliged to go back
in history—in this case to Paul's experience of transcendence in
1 Corinthians (2:9, 10). In each example, the questions posed
by parody and irony are formed by Paul's assertion that 'eye
hath not seen, nor ear heard . . . the things which God hath
prepared for them that love him'.

Once more we are obliged to hold past and present in a
double focus. This, the means of relativizing or 'transcending'
the present, is also the means of recalling what has been forgot-
ten or suppressed, and of freeing us from enslavement to the
immediate past. Without this sense of history, imagination
cannot fructify. Successful metaphors, for example, are never
wholly 'discontinuous'. Words retain their meanings, whether
we intend them or not; and we can no more be liberated from
their history than could Stephen Dedalus.

Although, as Lévi-Strauss has remarked, primitive life is a
luxury we can no longer afford, the further we move from past
levels of experience and intensities of sensibility, the greater
seems our preoccupation with them, and with the words they
gave us—such as God and conscience, which, since they are
used for experiences that are irreducible are themselves uninvertible. And since the metaphoric form is here inseparable
from the reality it renders intelligible, this is to move from the
'literary' to the 'religious' use of language. But to hold that the
experience of 'God' cannot be reduced to anything else, and the
word itself cannot be explained away, is not to assert that our
use of it is not, to some extent, a corrigible projection of a
particular culture, class, or temperament. The metaphors and
symbols which have traditionally expressed such experiences
are not wholly *aberglaube* or anthropomorphisms: they cannot
be reduced to adjectives, but remain words for which no further
expressions are ever fully adequate.[13] We have no other words

[13] See Alasdair MacIntyre's *Secularization and Moral Change*, Oxford, 1967, p. 69, for
another way of putting this point. The Arnoldian echo is significant: 'The suggestion
which I have made in these lectures that we cannot do with Christianity in the modern
world, but often cannot do without it entirely either, because we have no other
vocabulary in which to raise certain kinds of questions, could be framed once more in
terms of our inability to respond to the facts of death.'

to use. They succeed to the extent that they direct us to 'ultimate points of vision'. Arnold was right to locate the life-giving element in the imagination; but it is Coleridge who more exactly defines what such a location involves by emphasizing the purpose of imaginative 'diffusion' and 'dissipation'. It is in order to re-create, that is, to release new meanings by dissipating old ones; and we accept 'continuity' when we assume that the language retains the capacity to penetrate to 'the thing signified'. But the religious use of a language requires equally that old meanings shall be conserved. Cultic metaphors or 'signs' cannot be separated from the reality they render intelligible: the literal meaning is the figurative—God both is and is not our Father, and Jesus his son:

The cult-man stands alone in Pellam's land: more precariously than he knows he guards the *signa*: the pontifex among his house-treasures, (the twin *urbes* his house is) he can fetch things new and old. . . . This man, so late in time, curiously surviving, shows courtesy to the objects when he moves among, handles or puts aside the name-bearing instruments.[14]

As permanent and persistent metaphors, such 'signs' are the unparaphrasable element whose use in a poem, play, or novel either gives density or substance to metaphor and character, or, if unsuccessful, never rises above cliché. It is then that 'dead symbols litter to the base of the cult-stone'.[15] Even so, our understanding of the signs and symbols denoting ultimate points of vision is a function of their history. To reduce them to something else is to do more than render them meaningless, it is to reduce the dimensions of the public language; and a secular vocabulary which favours radical reduction at the expense of conservation (revealed in the crude opposition of *radical* as good, and *conservative* as bad) will never effect a resolution, only perpetuate an unresolved dilemma of two worlds in which, because we assume the old one to be dead, the new one becomes powerless to be born. If we seek liberation, it is the terms of the choice we must revise. To paraphrase Coleridge, we must perhaps conceive the old world and its meanings as the olive, and the new world and its meanings as the vine: the vine can grow without the olive, but it cannot fructify.

[14] David Jones, *The Anathemata*, London, 1952, p. 50.
[15] Ibid.

For example, when theologians and literary critics meet to discuss modern translations of the Bible, a similar distinction needs to be made between two needs or uses of language in scripture. The biblical theologian is concerned to press questions of truth, to establish with as great a degree of accuracy as possible what is being said, what actually happened, and, therefore, what we are to believe. His tendency is either to reduce or to expand the original in order to provide a satisfactory explanation. The translators of the Authorized Version knew where they stood dogmatically and, therefore, where their readers *ought* to stand; and it is this theological self-confidence which accounts for the substantiality of their use of metaphor. In the assertion 'I am the Resurrection and the Life', the figurative sense is the literal sense; and that is the measure of their success as translators. The translators of the New English Bible addressed themselves to the different needs of a 'generation less well educated than formerly . . . who do not go to church'.

Their translation conflicts with the use implicit in the demands made by literary critics. In the Authorized Version certain expressions have become, in the sense already defined, ultimate points of vision. They 'find' us. In referring to the 1662 burial service and to the passage from Job 14 beginning 'Man that is born of woman hath but a short time to live', Ian Robinson writes: 'As for the prayer, I, who am not a Christian, feel that it expresses exactly the truth I would like to find at that moment.'[16] Here the use required of scripture (and of its translation) differs from that of the biblical theologian, strictly speaking. It is ultimately and implicitly a doxological or liturgical use: it canonizes words for which we have no further or more adequate expression.

A modern translation of the Bible, to the extent to which it is helpful to the theologian or to the unbeliever, may cease to be as helpful to the worshipper, if it cannot be as effectively 'read aloud in the Churches' as can the Authorized Version. This brings me to Eliot's question[17]—should we speak of language as

[16] Ian Robinson, *The Survival of English*, Cambridge, 1973, p. 50.

[17] In D. Nineham, ed., *The New English Bible Reviewed*, London, 1965, p. 100. Cp. Newman's letter of 30 Aug. 1831, questioning Keble's presupposition that the English version of the Psalms could be made 'a fitter book of public worship by correcting its *style* and manner by the original': '*As they* are, we are habituated to them' (*Letters*, ii. 355–6).

having changed, or as having deteriorated? Conceptual distinctness can be gained at the expense of ineffable simplicity; and the demand that the Bible ought to be translated into literature may preserve, instinctively, a proper priority—that translations (and beliefs) are but inferences from more rudimentary forms of language. As Maurice remarks,[18] the language of scripture (as of the Creeds) must be placed 'in the midst of confessions, prayers, thanksgivings, which interpret its use', and, therefore, its meaning. The literary use is rudimental, and prior to the conceptual.

This controversy over modern translations of scripture is a prime example of how inevitable is the overlap of theology and literary criticism, and how unavoidable. In thus being brought to bear upon a common problem, each corrects the other; and to be able to recognize the overlap for what it is may help to remove inhibitions, on the critical side, of belief, and, on the theological side, of imaginative responsiveness.

As we have seen, because of its obligations to truth and fellowship, a religion can be reduced, easily and imperceptibly, to notions and loyalties; but when its mystique has been thus reduced, we discover that its God has become too small. To counteract such circumstances, the believer may resort to poetry as a substitute for the missing element in his religion—evidence that religion is, for the moment, dead to imagination and that what is, of its nature, 'a gift and a rarity' has become 'biassed and degraded by prejudice, passion and self interest'.[19] Passion and prejudice are the reverse side of imagination; and when they take over a religion, what is thus reduced to notions and clichés may remain alive only in poetry: it is then that poetry legitimately becomes our mysticism—a condition of which Newman was as aware as Arnold.[20] In such circumstances 'piety' may become what George Eliot perceptively refers to as a mere 'doctrinal transaction'.[21]

---

[18] See above, pp. 38ff.

[19] *GA*, pp. 251–2.

[20] *ECH* i. 290–1.

[21] 'He had long poured out utterances of repentance. But today a repentance had come which was of a bitterer flavour, and a threatening Providence urged him to a kind of propitiation which was not simply a doctrinal transaction. The divine tribunal had changed its aspect for him; self-prostration was no longer enough, and he must bring restitution in his hand' (George Eliot, *Middlemarch*, Oxford, 1950, chap. lxi, p. 665).

As in literature, so in religion, if our response is not to be a bland rhetorical gesture, it must signalize that intolerable wrestle with meaning, that sense not so much of dialectical pressure, as more properly of 'cruxifixion', which is at once a sign of literary and religious integrity. This may be why, in works of literature which deal with religion, indications of literary inadequacy seem to imply a corresponding religious inadequacy, and literary adequacy seems to guarantee its equivalent in religion.

(II) THE AUTHORITY OF METAPHOR AND SYMBOL

The extent of the grammar common to criticism and theology is revealed directly we notice that how we respond in literature to the ambiguities unified by metaphor is how, initially, we must respond to certain aspects of scripture and dogma. In each case the mode of operation is similar, so that the growth of literary judgement appears similar in form to being made by a religion. In as much as the successful literary critic lives all the metaphors he has assimilated,[22] so the believer is made by his religion as he succeeds in assimilating apparently discordant virtues: we are perpetually enjoined to be as harmless as doves, and as cunning as serpents, and to bring forth treasure which is both old and new. In Matthew 13:52, for example, Christ, after having spoken in a series of parables, is asked why he does so. His reply—that it is because the people do not understand him—seems as if he wishes to make himself deliberately difficult. He goes on to say that the Kingdom of Heaven is like a grain of mustard seed, and then, before we have had time to reflect, that it is a leaven, a pearl, and a treasure. This way of talking seems deliberately chosen to keep us from settling into a single, obsessive image—or a single, obsessive virtue; and in each case it is imagination which safeguards us from fixation. Historically, religion has always been afflicted by hard, unimaginative men whose practice of the single virtues of temperance, chastity, or humility has become fixated into total abstinence, sexual repression, or spineless passivity or accidie.

The enemy is fixation—in single virtues. The reward is a unity, found only at depth, like the bottom of the sea in a storm.[23] Yet we must take the risk, make the wager, and stand

---

[22] L. C. Knights, *Further Explorations*, London, 1965, p. 184.
[23] Newman: *PPS* v. 65ff.

out over 70,000 fathoms. These ways of putting the condition (by Pascal and Kierkegaard) take us back to the second part of this book, since our condition now is to begin deep within 'projections' (in the Feuerbachian sense), which have to be lived *with* to be lived *through*. Examples abound in the recent history of the spiritual life: like Stephen Dedalus, St. Teresa of Lisieux believed herself to be 'perfect' at the age of 13 and had to live through such pious projections in order to attain a true sanctity. Both von Hügel and the subject of his great work, St. Catherine of Genoa, began as damaged personalities—as more like a Sir Clifford Chatterley or a Dorothea Brooke, than a confident Lawrentian master of life.

As with the development of literary taste in the adolescent, so with the believer: each begins with signs and symbols which, subsequently, he may have to recognize as immature projections: as Eliot shows in *Four Quartets*, we start by understanding that what we ought to feel is conditional upon our feeling (and recognizing) our unsatisfactoriness for what it is. The next stage, as with the development of literary taste, is social: wider, more developed responsiveness is gained as we participate in the critical community, on the one hand, and in the historically continuous community, on the other. St. Catherine made herself in her work in the hospital she founded, where 'patients' were treated as the 'persons' they might become. Similarly, von Hügel laboured to keep the Church open and unsectarian in the midst of that crisis of authority and faith known as Modernism.

As with the growth to certitude, so with the development of literary judgement: each seeks fulfilment within a social framework or community. Each accepts an external authority as the essential *negative* curb to responses which, to the extent that they are merely subjective, are unreliable, inauthentic, or merely paradoxical. This is also to discover a parallel between building up the critical community on the one hand, and establishing the local church by public worship (or the liturgy) on the other. Thus to understand how the critical community is nourished, modified, and developed might lead us better to understand how to nourish, modify, and develop the local church. Much recent theology has been concerned with what might be called the theological form of the question: how can the liturgy be said to convert a local congregation into the church? What might be

called the secular form of the question is: if 'the literary-critical
judgement is the type of all judgements and valuations belonging to . . . the collaboratively created human world . . . which
is *neither* public . . . *nor* merely private and personal', how, in a
plural, permissive, and potentially dissociative society can we
possess and retain this 'third realm',[24] 'this third holy ground',
this meeting ground of 'the old dances and rituals'?

Leavis sees the university as pre-eminently such 'a real and
vital centre of consciousness . . . being in that way one of the
sustaining creative nuclei of a larger community'.

I have deliberately quoted the descriptions of such social
frameworks as they occur in Leavis and D. H. Lawrence respectively, since it is from theirs—the secular side—that the
question should first be pressed. But they, too, are left with
further questions: how does a community, which creates itself
by what it responds to, remain in growth? And if, like the
inerrant word of Scripture, it is the text which proves, what is
the *teaching* which is proven?

The theologian has been here before; in history, many times
before. To rest securely upon such assumptions, the funda-
mentalist critic must assume a fixed and stable teaching and
social order in which terms like 'life' and 'health'; 'vital' and
'vulgar'; 'debased' and 'stereotyped' can be referred to as self-
evident values. Historically, where such values are self-evident
and find their richest and most characteristic expression is in
the liturgy and literature of the age of Shakespeare. Thus, most
of the literature which is normative to such critical positions
derives from a pre-industrial society, which is organic and
neither pluralist nor 'hermeneutically indecisive', but is reinforced by liturgical and scriptural forms. The theologian's service to literary criticism is to show *how* this remains the case
even in later literature, particularly in the nineteenth century.
Thus he shows how Hardy's is a religious (and not unbelieving)
imagination, and how what is regarded as a literature of unbelief in that period is in fact literature of the contested religious
imagination, particularly when George Eliot is read alongside
Feuerbach and Strauss. By thus helping to characterize more
fully and accurately the affirmation or point of departure, the

---

[24] F. R. Leavis, *Lectures in America*, London, 1969, pp. 24–5, referring to a letter by
D. H. Lawrence of 11 Oct. 1926.

theologian may also be able to show how, for example, Arnold's poetry more adequately expresses his religion than his theological prose.

We can, of course, live by signs and symbols unreflectingly and unconsciously. We can be haunted by no intellectual perplexities, but directly we are, and the truth is troubled, the theologian is professionally of help. Living sacramentally—by metaphors, analogues, stories, or myths—has a history: it is the history of a religion. And what that history shows is that you cannot succeed in living *simply* by such signs for very long. They become implausible socially or metaphysically; and the history of theology is the history of the ways and means by which their integrity is preserved from the various forms of excess—institutional and legal, idolatrous and fanatical. The literary form of the question—how is the critical community formed and maintained?—has, as I have said, a theological form—how is the local church created and maintained? If what is true of the critical community—that it creates itself by what it responds to imaginatively—then the church likewise creates itself by what it responds to doxologically, viz., in the liturgy. It brings itself into being as it uses the language of eucharistic commemoration—'the future is realised in the present on the foundations of the past'.[25] It is in this sense that the local church may be spoken of as what 'has come down to us, not risen up among us, (being) found rather than established'.[26]

Yet to conceive the local church in this way requires a sharp imaginative shift and diffusion of perspective. We have to see that the idea of simple parochial location has gone with the society that made it possible, and that this trend cannot be resisted any more than the industrialization which occasioned it. To resist is merely to convert the church into a club, and Christian membership into one more club membership. The church is never a corner shop which has fallen into the wrong hands. Nor is it simply a matter of sacking the management and all will be well. This is to forget what lies behind Tertullian's warning repeated by Pascal that the Church is irreformable.

What, then, is it to be a Christian: what is Christian member-

---

[25] Oscar Cullmann, cited by I. H. Dalmais in *True Worship*, ed. L. Sheppard, the fifth Downside Symposium, London, 1963, p. 10.
[26] Newman, *Historical Sketches*, ii. 388.

ship? What follows from the disappearance of the territorial or parochial dimension is something wider and socially discontinuous. People come and go, yet remain more closely related than mere acquaintances. This, a fact of modern social life, has yet to be accepted as a relgous fact also. If the conception of membership is no longer territorial and ideological, then it returns to its origins, and becomes linguistic. As in the past, so now: the Christian is one who puts himself within an order of signs. Christians are those who separate themselves from the world by speaking and responding to a common language. It is formed (and re-formed) by the liturgy—'the table of God's word'[27]—nourished by scripture (and therefore analogical), and completed in the living out of what it enjoins. Theologically, it is a language which appeals *through* imagination, *with* reason, *to* the conscience. Poetically, it is resolved in Yeats's question, thus:

> How but in custom and in ceremony
> Are innocence and beauty born?
> (Yeats: *Prayer for my daughter*)

Membership of the Church is in fact chiefly to be recognized (and respected) today as of those who talk and act in ways peculiar to their language and its forms: members are identified by a certain kind of moral style, for which they have a vocabulary of their own: 'that new language which Christ has brought us'. They wait patiently in faith and hope, act charitably to all, and treat their bodies as the temples of an in-dwelling spirit. Even when paraphrased or modified, this characteristic oddness remains. Yet, as Bonhoeffer has argued and shown in the manner of his death, instead of keeping religious and secular meanings apart, we should be seeking their resolution in a common language. Otherwise, religious meanings will fade from daily use. We cannot afford Tyrrell's despair, or Barth's, or even (to a lesser extent) Maurice's—that between the language of God and that of men there is an absolute qualitative distinction. Instead, once more, it is the poets to whom we must turn

[27] See *Documents of Vatican II*, ed. Abbott, London, 1966. *Dei Verbum* (*Constitution on Divine Revelation*), vi. 21: 'The Church has always venerated the divine scriptures just as she venerates the body of the Lord, since from the table of both the word of God and of the body of Christ she unceasingly receives and offers to the faithful the bread of life, *especially* in the sacred liturgy.' Cp. *Constitution on the Liturgy*, ii. 51, which also refers to 'the table of God's Word'.

for the true description of our condition. It is that of a Night Battle—where friend and foe stand together, and membership of the household of faith is as much evident in remaining within these forms of faith, or universes of discourse, as in 'attending' church. Thus it is that we are already more prepared to listen to those who would speak with us (but are unable to 'believe' or 'worship' with us); and we are also changing our attitudes to those (often our own children) who are 'lapsed', but still talk a common language, using its vocabulary for their moral expectations. Perhaps we are unconsciously developing the ancient notion of 'hierarchy', and discovering that there are degrees of belonging to the church: some, by virtue of office or profession, being more fully in membership, than others who are not necessarily out of membership.

Our children press on with questions we are still too hard-headed to answer: are the grounds any longer sufficient for us to remain divided as Christians? Or do our divisions rest upon distinctions, once held to be theological, but now seen to be determined by (and persisted in from) unconsciously suppressed social and political preferences? Have these diminished our proper (because imaginative) response to the Scriptures, which serve to call us out of a world grown too familiar?

Hitherto, believers have resisted plurality and diversity, conceiving them to be a threat to unity because incompatible with it. Thus they have attempted to reduce their internal contradictions and external differences either to a uniformity which can be affirmed, and a counter-position that can be defended, or to a heresy that can be repudiated; and their institutions have had this character too—that of being counter-societies.

A plural society, however, presses them to accept a new kind of asceticism—'institutional' and 'legal'—and this is already evident in the churches. Their members are now much less able to build counter-societies, since circumstances inevitably destine these to be even more rapidly superseded than in the past. But pluralism requires more than abstention and toleration, since a religion in which the imaginative power to diffuse and dissipate inherited notions and customs is inhibited does more than breed sectarian fanaticism. Its dogmatic or rudimentary forms lose plausibility and meaning. The contribution of believers to a plural society lies in giving secular meanings to religious assertions. In the circumstances of the class war and racial discrimination, for example, it lies in showing how, by means of the redemptive work of Christ, we are *already* members one of another; and that our unity, far from having to be gained by successful polemic or bloody revolution, has but to be discovered, realized and proclaimed. In this we would be carrying out the prophetic vision of an F.D. Maurice in England, and a Vladimir Solovyev in Russia.

In religion, imagination when suppressed encourages hard-headedness and permits fanaticism; but in literature, when socially unchecked and unformed, it evaporates into purest subjectivity. In religion, the signs and symbols which direct a life of virtue are held doxologically or liturgically; and this origin and proper placing in the public prayer of the Church is the source of their power to authenticate. Historically, as I have argued, it was from this religious *praxis* that the literary imagination derived its shape, density, and authority. As this influence diminished, the density of metaphor and its power to convince weakened, as may be seen when the metaphorical power of *Lear* is compared with that of *The Scholar-Gipsy*.[28]

What literature gains from theology is a model for its self-understanding—how its metaphors succeed in gaining *authority*: successful metaphors, like religious analogues, are deeply rooted, historically, in the public language. To assume that the historical relation between imagination and religion is an accident merely of time and place, and that it will be superseded by an autonomous imagination is a mistake which literary critics themselves rarely make in practice. In the passage already quoted,[29] Matthew Arnold certainly seems to prophesy that imagination alone will now perform what in the past was gained from the imaginative grasp of the symbols, rites, ethics, and institutions of religion. This prophecy was made a hundred years ago. Since then, we have had Joyce and Beckett, but we have also had Eliot and Pasternak. Imagination remains supersaturated with religion; and if we concede Arnold's claim that the strongest part of our religion is its unconscious poetry, can we not also assert that the strongest part of our poetry is its unconscious religion? There may be neither an autonomous nor a purely secular imagination. The development of the literary

[28] See above, pp. 24ff.   [29] See above, p. 97.

critical judgement, like the religious, is a social growth, and one
which requires reliable inferences, if the metaphors it responds
to are to become an authentic source of a way of life. The source
of authority in each case is a praxis socially conceived: we live
by reliable inferences which we trust to converge into beliefs. In
each case we face Newman's question[30]—how do I know that
there is something real to correspond to my convictions; and
what authorizes them? Are the signs *authentic*?

We have already seen how the Church completes this
authenticating function for Newman.[31] The university, for
Leavis, performs the same function, since to conceive it as
where the critical community creates itself by what it responds
to, in order to become thereby the nucleus of the larger
community, is to describe analogously how the Church is
established by the liturgy. Furthermore, this is a conception of
the university which presumes that the separate disciplines are,
in tendency, integrative and converging, not dissociative—a
tendency which although appearing always at risk is always
sustained by the university's innate capacity to remain a
community.

Thus the university, like the Church for Newman, is in its
idea a source of authority.[32] It is a community whose function is
to bring the convictions of its members to trial, accepting them
only in so far as they are imaginative, reasonable, and reliably
to be acted upon. Such are the means by which standards of
criticism are maintained and transmitted. What is further presupposed is 'a whole existing order'—or tradition—which, accepted as trustworthy and authentic, is communicated only in
so far as it is successfully modified, adapted, and developed. In
so far as to seek imaginative credibility is part of the obligation
to believe, so to research is (for like reason) part of the obligation to teach.

The objector may urge, however, that although this may still
be true of the university, at least in its *idea*—as it was, of course,
for Newman, and as it has been for Leavis—it cannot be true of
tradition as it is understood by the Church. I have argued that
tradition as the Church understands it is, in the literary sense,
'a form of faith', and that it is literary criticism which has
preserved the best understanding of the forms which manifest

[30] See above, p. 54.   [31] See above, p. 78f.   [32] See above, p. 80.

continuity within tradition. This is because such forms are *primarily* symbolic (and therefore imaginative and literary). They are conceptually conceivable only in so far as they are effectively symbolic and imaginatively credible: this is the source of the secret discipline for which Bonhoeffer was prepared to die. But it is not so much a new insight as a rediscovery. The ancient term for creed, *symbolum*, for example, marks both its symbolic and performative character,[33] and the 'rudimental' forms of tradition, although 'dilated' in scripture, are 'contracted' in the Creed.[34] Thus, as we should expect, there has been an integral relation between symbol and its explanation in the Church's formulation of its dogmas; and it is plausible to accept the view that the Church's strong objections to defective or contrary formulations 'have rested on the conviction that the integrity of the images or symbols which dominate a man's soul is of the utmost importance to his own well-being'. What he thinks or says about them matters because they mediate 'a healing or saving truth'.[35] A difficulty now arises for theologians which does not worry literary critics. To conceive continuity within tradition as appealing in the first instance to symbolic imagination rather than to rational definition is to seem to be in danger of dealing with irresolvable contradictions and dissociating diversities. Well may Coleridge describe the power of imagination as revealing itself 'in the balance or reconcilement of opposite or discordant qualities'.[36] This may make for a good novel or a dramatic poem, but it does not seem to suggest an effective method for the handing on of beliefs from one generation to the next. By reminding us of the problems which Newman was concerned to resolve, this objection also demonstrates why it is Newman's formulation of the question which alone makes possible its resolution. If we wish to know how to perpetuate our beliefs through change, we must first discover how what begins as 'an impression upon the Imagination' becomes 'a system or creed in the reason'. In other words we must discover how to achieve the difficult resolution of faith into belief.

[33] '. . . on the analogy of the pacts or agreements which business men enter into with one another': St. Augustine cited by J. N. D. Kelly, *Early Christian Creeds*, London, 1960, p. 55.

[34] Newman: *VM* i. 230; ii. 278; see above, p. 37.

[35] V. White, *Soul and Psyche*, p. 91.   [36] *BL*, p. 151.

CONCLUSION

7

The Difficult Resolution

Newman's question invites us to distinguish faith from belief, while the form taken by religious imagination in the nineteenth century, and later, invites us to attempt their difficult resolution. But, as we have seen, faith and belief refer, not to different things but to the same thing in different stages of our awareness. Thus the distinction is between implicit and explicit, between the initial creative, but as yet indeterminate, act of assent, and its articulation conceptually.

This is a distinction to recognize but not to press, otherwise we forget that sometimes, as when we refer to the Fatherhood of God, a theological notion and a religious reality may be expressed by the same proposition, while serving 'as distinct interpretations of it'.[1] The object of our assent lies hid in language; and it is only if we inhibit a full response to the language of imagination that we are predisposed to deny that faith can be transformed into belief. Once we accept that faith and belief originate in a common grammar, we are as much entitled as in the past to hold more than we can explain or rationally verify. We can continue to trust that our saying and unsaying need not remain unresolved, but can lead to a positive result; and that by becoming 'too powerful and concurrent for refutation' the probabilities of faith will grow into that greater discursive adequacy we know as 'belief'.

Although Newman is justified in asserting it to be a fact that probabilities converge into certitude, he admits that there can be no absolute tests of false certitude and true; and we must recognize that the model used is that of the action of grace as when, for example, faith achieves understanding in 'the midst of confessions, prayers, and thanksgivings', and our investiga-

[1] *GA*, p. 91, see above, p. 41.

tions are fulfilled as we are enabled to 'pray the unprayable prayer'. Newman's argument requires, in the end, 'the interposition of a Power greater than human teaching and human argument to make our beliefs true and our minds one'.[2] So that although the grounds on which we authenticate our assents remain 'outside the chain of cause and effect', how they do so remains as much a mystery for us as they are for Levin (at the end of *Anna Karenina*) or for Newman himself.

Since the mystery we assent to is articulated in the paradoxes of Incarnation, it is experienced as an incomprehensible certitude; and we can never hope to live without questions, therefore. In Barth's words our experience is of 'a central void (in which) the answer to our questioning is hidden; but since the void is defined by questions, they must never for one moment cease'.[3] It is for this reason that, although we may come 'to know that we know', our firm assent is to what is *obscurely* revealed, and the difficult resolution of faith into belief, once achieved, can go out of focus and degenerate into cliché. Although certitudes endure, therefore, assents change as each generation discovers when, in exercising its religious imagination, it realizes that it can neither live with the beliefs it has inherited, nor live without them.

The theologian is wise if he seeks the renewal of belief where poetry and religion modulate into each other; and, in a manner akin to the literary critic, if he is to make a real assent to the objects of faith, the theologian must 'use his imagination', which means undertaking the intolerable wrestle with meaning, since what he seeks to renew lies 'hid in language'. But whereas the literary critic seeks assents which, as he responds to the best words in the best order, or to the proper ordering of the questions by a Shakespeare or a Dostoevsky, first suspend his disbelief, and then predispose him to believe in the reality of what they 'imagine', the theologian goes further. He seeks imaginative assents which are convertible into certitudes, since his assumption is that what his beliefs refer to perpetuates its identity through change. Yet in each case it is the achievement of linguistic adequacy—the avoidance of cliché—which seems to guarantee the adequacy of the experience, and of the meaning we give it.

[2] *GA*, p. 285.   [3] *The Epistle to the Romans*, p. 254.

If, as I have argued, Eliot's method as a poet, and its theological implications, are most fully expressed by Newman (in the *Grammar of Assent* as supplemented by the Notebooks and other writings), then the value to the theologian of Newman's work lies in the soundness and integrity of its *literary* method, that is, in its sensitivity to the language of imagination. No concessions are made either to the over-confidence of an unlettered theology, or to the modernist despair that the symbolic forms of faith are incompatible with and inexpressible in the language of belief. Conversely, Eliot's poetry exemplifies what Newman's theology explains; and if Newman's is the grammar of the poetry, Eliot's is the poetry of the grammar. The poetry shows how we may hold imaginative assents which we can neither adequately explain nor demonstratively verify. A proper theology shows how, by saying and unsaying, such assents are authenticated and become beliefs which we are entitled to hold and to live by. This is what justifies the association of theologians and literary critics, suspicious but cousinly, in joint study. In opposition, each inhibits the other; together they uncover a common grammar.

Bibliography

I MANUSCRIPT SOURCES

Those papers, covering the years 1846–65, which deal with Newman's preparatory work for the *Grammar of Assent*. They are chiefly to
be found in the Birmingham Oratory archives in packets B.9.11,
B.7.4, A.23.1, and A.30.11, and are listed by Newman in a note of 30
October 1870, in *Autobiographical Writings*, pp. 269f.

II BOOKS AND PERIODICALS

Note: Place of publication London, unless otherwise stated.

ANDREWES, Lancelot (Bishop). *Ninety-six Sermons*, 5 vols., Oxford,
   1841–3.
—— *Preces Privatae*, ed. F. E. Brightman, 1903.
—— See also, Mozley, J. B.; and Eliot, T. S., *Selected Essays.*
ARNOLD, Matthew. *Poetical Works*, 1891.
—— *The Notebooks of*, ed. H. F. Lowry, K. Young, and W. H. Dunn,
   Oxford, 1952.
—— *St. Paul and Protestantism*, 1870.
—— *Literature and Dogma* (1873), 1891.
—— *God and the Bible*, 1875.
—— *Last Essays on Church and Religion*, 1877.
—— *Essays in Criticism*, first and second series, 1865, 1888.
—— *Mixed Essays* (1879), 1880.
AUERBACH, Erich. *Mimesis*, Princeton, 1968.
BAILLIE, J. See Eliot, T. S. (c).
BARTH, Karl. *The Epistle to the Romans*, translated from the sixth
   edition by Edwyn C. Hoskyns, 1968.
BERGER, Peter. *A Rumour of Angels*, 1971.
BLAKE, William. *The Poetical Works*, ed. John Sampson, Oxford, 1943.
BLONDEL, Maurice. *Letter on Apologetics* and *History and Dogma*, E. T.
   Alexander Dru and Dom Illtyd Trethowan, 1964.
BONHOEFFER, Dietrich. *Letters and Papers from Prison*, 1959.
—— *Lectures on Christology* (1960), E.T. Edwin Robertson, 1978.
BRADLEY, F.H. *Appearance and Reality*, 1893.
—— *Ethical Studies*, Oxford, 1927.

BRAITHWAITE, R. B. *An Empiricist's View of the Nature of Religious Belief*, Cambridge, 1955.

BULTMANN, Rudolf. *Existence and Faith*, E.T., 1964.

BUTLER, Joseph. *The Analogy of Religion* (1736), ed. Samuel Halifax, 1834.

CHEKHOV, Anton. *The Selected Letters of Anton Chekhov*, ed. L. Hellman, 1955.

CHURCH, R. W. *The Oxford Movement, Twelve Years 1833–1845*, 1891.

—— *Life and Letters of*, ed. Mary C. Church, 1895.

COLERIDGE, S. T. *Collected Letters of Samuel Taylor Coleridge*, ed. E. L. Griggs, 6 vols., Oxford, 1956–71.

—— *The Notebooks of Samuel Taylor Coleridge*, ed. Kathleen Coburn, 3 vols., 1957– .

—— *The Table Talk and Omniana of Samuel Taylor Coleridge*, Oxford, 1917.

—— *The Friend, a series of Essays* (1809–10), ed. Barbara E. Rooke, *Collected Works*, vol. iv, 1969.

—— *Lay Sermons*, ed. R. J. White, *Collected Works*, vol. vi, 1972.

—— *Biographia Literaria* (1817; 2nd edn. 1847), Everyman edn., 1952.

—— *Aids to Reflection* (1825) and *The Confessions of an Inquiring Spirit* (1840), Bohn, 1904.

—— *The Literary Remains of Samuel Taylor Coleridge*, ed. H. N. Coleridge, 4 vols., 1836–9.

—— *Shakespearean Criticism*, ed. T. M. Raysor, 2 vols., Everyman edn., 1960.

CONGAR, Y. *Tradition and Traditions* (1963), E.T., 1966.

COULSON, J. *Newman and the Common Tradition*, Oxford, 1970.

—— See Newman, J. H. (c).

DALY, Gabriel. *Transcendence and Immanence, A Study in Catholic Modernism and Integralism*, Clarendon Press, Oxford, 1980.

DANTE. *Epistolae* X, 'Letter to Can Grande', E.T. Temple Classics, 1904.

DENZINGER, H. *Enchiridion Symbolorum . . . de rebus fidei et morum*, Friburgi Brisgoviae: Herder, 1947.

DICKENS, Charles. *Hard Times*, 1854.

DILLISTONE, F. W. *The Christian understanding of Atonement*, 1968.

—— *Traditional Symbols and the Contemporary World*, 1973.

DISRAELI, B. *Sybil, or the Two Nations*, 1845.

DONNE, John. *The Sermons*, ed. G. R. Potter and E. M. Simpson, 10 vols., California U.P., 1953–62.

DOSTOEVSKY, F. M. *Crime and Punishment* (1866), E.T. Penguin, 1966.

—— *The Brothers Karamazov* (1880), E.T. Penguin, 1958, 2 vols.

—— *Letters of F. M. Dostoevsky to his family and friends*, ed. Mayne, E.T., 1962.

DOWNSIDE SYMPOSIA. See Kent; Sheppard.

ELIOT, George. *Adam Bede* (1859), Everyman edn., 1960.
—— *Felix Holt* (1866), Everyman edn., 1964.
—— *Middlemarch* (1872), Oxford, 1950.
—— *George Eliot's Life related in her Letters and Journals*, ed. J. W. Cross, 1885.

ELIOT, T. S.
(a) POETRY: *Four Quartets* (1935–42), 1944. *Collected Poems* (1909–62), 1963. See Gardner, Helen.
(b) CRITICISM: *The Idea of a Christian Society*, 1939. *Notes towards the Definition of Culture*, 1948. *Selected Essays* (1932) 3rd edn., 1969. *On Poetry and Poets* (1957), 1971.
(c) CONTRIBUTIONS TO BOOKS AND PERIODICALS: *The Criterion*, vol. iv, Oct. 1926, pp. 751–7, review of Ramon Fernandez, *Messages*, in which Eliot sums up a discussion on Newman begun in the issue for Oct. 1924: *The experience of Newman*, Ramon Fernandez, vol. iii, Oct. 1924, pp. 84–102; *A French criticism of Newman*, Frederic Manning, vol. iv, Jan. 1926, pp. 19–31; *The experience of Newman: reply to Frederic Manning*, Ramon Fernandez, vol. iv, Oct. 1926, pp. 645–58. *The Enemy*, Jan. 1927, 'A Note on Poetry and Belief.' *The Dial*, Feb. 1928. 'An Emotional Unity'. *The Listener*, 16 Mar. 1932. *Revelation*, ed. John Baillie and Hugh Martin, 1937. *The New English Bible Reviewed*, ed. D. Nineham, 1965.

ENGELS, F. See Marx, K.

FERNANDEZ, R. See Eliot, T. S. (c).

FEUERBACH, Ludwig. *The Essence of Christianity* (E.T. George Eliot, 1854), New York, Torchbooks, 1957.

FITZGERALD, C. Scott. *Tender is the Night*, the Bodley Head edn. of Scott Fitzgerald, vol. ii, the original 1934 version, 3rd impression 1973.

GARDNER, Helen. *Religion and Literature*, 1971.
—— *The Composition of Four Quartets*, 1978.

HAMPSHIRE, Stuart. In *The Morality of Scholarship*, ed. Max Black, New York, 1967.

HARDY, Thomas. *The Woodlanders*, 1887.
—— *Jude the Obscure* (1895), 1923.
—— *The Dynasts*, 1903–8.
—— *Collected Poems*, 1932, incl. *Late Lyrics and Earlier* (1922).

HENSON, H. H. *The Church of England*, Cambridge, 1939.

HOPKINS, G. M. *Letters to Robert Bridges*, ed. C. C. Abbott, 2nd edn., 1955.
—— *Further Letters of G. M. Hopkins*, ed. C. C. Abbott, 2nd edn., 1956.

HÜGEL, F. von (Baron). *The Mystical Element of Religion as studied in St.*

Catherine of Genoa and her friends, 2 vols. (1908), 2nd edn., 1923.

—— *Eternal Life*, 1912.

—— *Selected Letters*, 1927.

HUIZINGA, J. *The Waning of the Middle Ages* (1924), 1955.

IBSEN, Henrik. *The Wild Duck*, (1884), E.T. U. Ellis-Fermor, 1950.

JOHNSON, Samuel. *Lives of the Poets* (1779–81), 2 vols., Oxford, 1906.

JONES, David. *The Anathemata*, 1952.

JOYCE, James. *A Portrait of the Artist as a Young Man* (1916), Penguin, 1964.

JUNG, C. G. *Psychology and Religion*, New Haven, Yale U.P., 1960.

KELLY, J. N. D. *Early Christian Creeds*, 1960.

KENT, J. and MURRAY, R. (edd.) *Intercommunion and Church Membership*, the Tenth Downside Symposium, 1973.

KHOMIAKOV, A. S. *L'Église Latine et la Protestantisme au point de vue de l'Église d'Orient*, Lausanne, 1872.

KIERKEGAARD, Soren. *The Journals of*, selected and translated A. Dru: (i) Oxford, 1939; (ii) New York, Torchbooks, 1959.

—— *Fear and Trembling* (1843) and *The Sickness unto Death* (1846), New York, Anchor, 1954.

—— *Concluding Unscientific Postscript* (1846), Princeton U.P., 1941.

—— *Of the Difference between a Genius and an Apostle* (1847), E.T. A. Dru, 1972.

KNIGHTS, L. C. *Further Explorations*, 1965.

KÜNG, Hans. *Justification*, 1964.

LASH, N. *Credal Affirmation as a criterion of Church Membership*, in the Tenth Downside Symposium, ed. Kent and Murray (q.v.).

LAWRENCE, D. H.

(a) NOVELS: *The Rainbow* (1915), 1970. *Women in Love* (1920), 1968. *Kangaroo* (1923), 1963. *St. Mawr* (1925), 1950. *The Man who died* (1929), 1960.

(b) LETTERS AND CRITICISM: *The Letters*, ed. Aldous Huxley, 1956. *Selected Essays*, ed. Richard Aldington, 1950. *Phoenix*, the posthumous papers, selections from, ed. A. H. Inglis, 1971. *Apocalypse* (1931), 1974.

LEAVIS, F. R. *New Bearings in English Poetry*, 1932.

—— *The Common Pursuit*, 1952.

—— *English Literature in our time and the University*, 1969.

—— *Lectures in America*, 1969.

LEUBA, Jean-Louis. *'L'Institution et L'Événement'*, *Les Deux Modes de l'oeuvre de Dieu selon le Nouveau Testament, leur différence, leur unité*, 1950; E.T. *New Testament Pattern*, 1953.

LEWIS, C. S. *De Descriptione Temporum*, in *They asked for a Paper* (1962).

LOISY, A. *The Gospel and the Church*, E.T. 1903.

LONERGAN, Bernard. *Method in Theology*, 1972.

MACINTYRE, A. *Secularization and Moral Change*, Oxford, 1967.

MANNING, H. E. *The Eternal Priesthood*, 17th edn., 1907.

MARCUSE, H. *One Dimensional Man*, 1968.

MARX, K. and ENGELS, F. *Basic Writings*, ed. L. S. Feuer, 1969.

MAURICE, F. D. *Subscription No Bondage, or the Practical Advantages afforded by the Thirty-Nine Articles as Guides in all the Branches of Academical Education*, by Rusticus, 1835.

—— *The Kingdom of Christ*, new edition based on the second edition of 1842, ed. Alec R. Vidler, 2 vols., 1958.

—— *Sermons on the Prayer Book, and the Lord's Prayer* (1848), 1893.

—— *The Epistles of St. John, a series of Lectures on Christian Ethics* (1857), 1881.

—— *What is Revelation? A series of sermons on the Epiphany: to which are added letters to a student of theology on the Bampton Lectures of Mr. Mansel*, 1859.

—— Maurice, Frederick, *The Life of Frederick Denison Maurice, chiefly told in his own letters*, 2 vols., 1884.

MILL, J. S. *Autobiography*, Oxford, 1949.

—— *Essays on Bentham and Coleridge* (1838; 1840), ed. F. R. Leavis, 1962.

MINNEAR, Paul S. *Images of the Church in the New Testament*, 1961.

MOZLEY, J. B. 'Bishop Andrewes' Sermons', *The British Critic*, vol. xxxi, no. 61, Jan. 1842.

MOZLEY, T. *Reminiscences of the Oxford Movement*, 2 vols., 1882.

NÉDONCELLE, M. *Le Chrétien appartient à deux mondes*, Paris, 1970.

NEWMAN, J. H.

(a) IN PUBLISHED WORKS: *The Arians of the Fourth Century* (1833), 1871. *Parochial and Plain Sermons*, 8 vols. (1834–43; republished 1868), 1877. *Select Treatises of St. Athanasius*, 2 vols., Oxford, 1842–4. *Fifteen Sermons preached before the University of Oxford* (1843), 1880. *An Essay on the Development of Christian Doctrine* (1845), ed. C. F. Harrold, New York, 1949. *Discourses addressed to Mixed Congregations* (1849), 1876. *Lectures on the Present Position of Catholics* (1851), Dublin, 1857. *Certain Difficulties felt by Anglicans in Catholic Teaching*, 2 vols., vol. i, 1850; vol. ii (including *Letter to the Duke of Norfolk*, 1875), 1876. *Apologia pro Vita Sua* (1864): (i) the two versions of 1864 and 1865, ed. Wilfrid Ward, Oxford, 1913; (ii) (new edn.), with introduction and notes by M. J. Svaglic, Oxford, 1967. *Verses on Various Occasions* (1868), 1903. *An Essay in aid of a Grammar of Assent* (1870), ed. C. F. Harrold, New York, 1947. *Essays Critical and Historical* (1871), 2 vols., 1890. *Historical Sketches* (1872), 3 vols. 1891; 1891; 1872. *Discussions and Arguments on Various Subjects*, 1872. *The Idea of a University defined and*

Illustrated (1873), 1925. *The Via Media of the Anglican Church* (1877), 2 vols., 1895, 1901.
(b) IN LETTERS, JOURNALS, AND NOTEBOOKS: *John Henry Newman: Autobiographical Writings*, ed. Henry Tristram, 1956. *Letters and Correspondence of John Henry Newman during his Life in the English Church*, ed. Anne Mozley, 1890–1. *The Letters and Diaries of John Henry Newman*, ed. Charles Stephen Dessain of the Birmingham Oratory, vols. xi (Oct. 1845) ff.; 1961—, in progress. *The Philosophical Notebook*, edited at the Birmingham Oratory by Edward Sillem and revised by A. J. Boekraad, vol. i, General Introduction, vol. ii, The Text, Editions Nauwelaerts, Louvain, 1970. *The Theological Papers of John Henry Newman on Faith and Certainty*, partly prepared for publication by Hugo M. de Achaval, S. J. Selected and edited by J. Derek Holmes with a note of introduction by Charles Stephen Dessain, Clarendon Press, 1976. *Newman the Oratorian, his Unpublished Oratory Papers*, ed. Placid Murray, Dublin, 1969.
(c) IN BIOGRAPHICAL AND RELATED SOURCES: Coulson, John, *Newman and the Common Tradition*, Oxford, 1970. Coulson, John and Allchin, A. M. *The Rediscovery of Newman*, An Oxford Symposium, 1967. Dessain, C. S. *John Henry Newman*, 1966. Ward, Wilfrid, *The Life of John Henry, Cardinal Newman*, based on his private journals and correspondence, 2 vols., 1921. See Eliot, T. S. (c).

NINEHAM, D. (ed.). See Eliot, T. S. (c).

OWEN, Wilfrid. *The Collected Poems*, ed. C. Day Lewis, 1963. See Stallworthy.

PATTISON, Mark. *Memoirs*, 1885.

PÉGUY, Charles. See Villiers, M.

PETRE, M. D. See Tyrrell.

PRICE, H. H. *Belief*, 1969.

RAHNER, K. 'Pluralism in Theology and the Unity of the Church's Profession of Faith', in *Concilium*, June 1969.

RICOEUR, Paul. *The Symbolism of Evil*, Boston, 1969.

ROBINSON, Ian. *The Survival of English*, Cambridge, 1973.

SCHLEIERMACHER, F. *On Religion Speeches addressed to its cultured despisers* (1799), E.T. 1893.

SCHLINK, E. *The Coming Christ and the Coming Church*, Edinburgh, 1967.

SHAKESPEARE, William. For the texts of *Macbeth, King Lear, A Winter's Tale*, see *The Collected Works*, ed. W. J. Craig, Oxford, 1943.

SHEPPARD, L. *True Worship*, ed. L. Sheppard, the Fifth Downside Symposium, 1963.

—— *Lacordaire, a biographical essay*, 1964.

SOLOVYEV, Vladimir. *Lectures on Godmanhood* (1877–84), E.T. 1948.

STALLWORTHY, Jon. *Wilfred Owen*, 1977.

STRAUSS, D. F. *Life of Jesus* (1835–6), E.T., 1974.

TOLSTOY, Leo. *Anna Karenina* (1878), E.T. 1954.

TURGENEV, Ivan. *Fathers and Sons* (1861), E.T. Penguin, 1965.

TUVE, R. *A Reading of George Herbert*, 1932.

TYRRELL, George. 'Hilaire Bourdon', *The Church and the Future*, 1903.

—— *Through Scylla and Charybdis*, 1907.

—— *Medievalism*, 1908.

—— *Christianity at the Cross Roads* (1909), 1963.

—— *Essays on Faith and Immortality*, 1914.

—— *Revelation as Experience*, first published in *The Heythrop Journal*, vol. xii, 1971.

—— *George Tyrrell's Letters*, ed. M. D. Petre, 1920.

—— Petre, M. D., *Autobiography and Life of George Tyrrell*, 2 vols., 1912.

VATICAN II, documents of. *Lumen Gentium* (*Dogmatic Constitution on the Church*); *Dei Verbum* (*Constitution on Divine Revelation*); *Sacrosanctum Concilium* (*Constitution on the Sacred Liturgy*). In *The Documents of Vatican II*, ed. Walter M. Abbott, 1966.

VIDLER, A. R. *The Modernist Movement in the Roman Church*, Cambridge, 1934.

VILLIERS, M. *Charles Péguy*, 1965.

WHITE, Victor. *Soul and Psyche*, 1959.

WILDER, Amos N. *Early Christian Rhetoric*, 1964.

WITTGENSTEIN, Ludwig. *Philosophical Investigations*, Oxford, 1953.

——*Remarks on the Foundation of Mathematics*, 1956.

WORDSWORTH, William. *The Prelude*, 1850.

—— *Preface* (1800) to Wordsworth and Coleridge, *Lyrical Ballads* (1798).

YEATS, W. B. *Later Poems*, 1922.

INDEX